A WESTERN SAMPLER

NINE CONTEMPORARY POETS

A

WESTERN SAMPLER

❋ ❋ ❋

Nine Contemporary Poets

Selected by the Editors of *Talisman*

❋ ❋ ❋

THE TALISMAN PRESS
Georgetown, California 1963

ACKNOWLEDGMENTS

Acknowledgment is made to the following for granting permission to publish poems included in this anthology.

ANN STANFORD: "Lost Objects," "Person and Place," originally published in *Poetry*. "The Walnuts," Hidden Things," first published in *The Hudson Review*. "Notes to go with a Compass," from *Choice*. "An Anniversary," from *Inland*. "The Riders" originally appeared in *Variegation*. "The Weathercock," "The Genie" originally published in *The Sewanee Review*. "The Bear" from *Epoch*. "Pastoral on the Back Nine," "The Pool" first appeared in *University of Kansas City Review*. "Night Piece," from *Yankee*. "Pandora" from *Coastlines*. "The Faces" from *Massachusetts Review*.

WILLIAM STAFFORD: "In Dear Detail, by Ideal Light," appeared in *Traveling Through the Dark*, copyright 1959 by William E. Stafford. Reprinted by permission of Harper & Row, publishers, 1962. "Return to Single Shot" appeared in *Poetry*. "Truth is the Only Way Home" from *Commonweal*. "Some Shadows" appeared in *Compass Review*. "A Diary Entry" from *December*. "A Documentary from America" first published in *Critical Review*.

HOWARD BAKER: "Ode to the Sea," "Pont Neuf" first published in *Letter From the Country*, New Directions. Reprinted by permission of the author. "The Old Actor to His Conscience," "The Fall of Miletus" by permission of the author.

CLINTON WILLIAMS: "Epistle for my Son" first appeared in *Quarterly Review of Literature*. "The Incorruptibles" from *Pacific Spectator*. "Vignette" appeared in *The Prairie Schooner*. "Poulenc's Carmelites," "Season Piece," "Two Friends" originally published in *Crocodile Review*.

MYRON BROOMELL: "Four Sonnets," "Lines for Ponce De Leon," reprinted from *The Time by Dialing* by Myron H. Broomell by permission of the publisher, Alan Swallow. "The City Built on Sand, Numbers 5, 10, 16" reprinted from *The City Built on Sand* by Myron H. Broomell by permission of the publisher, Alan Swallow. Copyright 1948 by Alan Swallow. "The Temporalities," "Of Novel Disseizin" appeared in *Poetry*. "We Must Write Often" from *Palisade*. "Landscape" from *Yankee*. "The Prank" from *New Mexico Quarterly Review*. "Directions" from

Arizona Quarterly. "On Being Too Busy to Attend One's Twenty-fifth Class Reunion," "An Unwritten Essay of Montaigne," "The Woman" published in *Yale Review.* "Landscape," "Of Novel Disseizin," "The Prank," "Directions," also appeared in *The Outdoor Labyrinth,* copyright by Myron Broomell and reprinted with permission of the author.

HAROLD WITT: "The Double Boy" appeared in *Carleton Miscellany.* "Hand on the Gun," "Some Lives," "Poets I Know" first appeared in *Poetry Northwest.* "From Aunts and Uncles 2 and 3," "Dreamscape in Kummel," originally published in *The New Yorker.* "Rushmore," "Dubuque," and "Inside Iowa" appeared in *The Hudson Review.* "Killer" from *Kenyon Review.* "The Noble Savage," reprinted from *The Death of Venus* by Harold Witt, reprinted by permission of Golden Quill Press.

ALAN STEPHENS: "Don Juan," "A Walk in the Void," "Urban Moral," "Written from a Grove," "Homily," "You Need a Change of Scene," "The Daimon's Advice," "The Sun," "Anniversary Sequence" reprinted from *The Sum* by Alan Stephens by permission of the publisher, Alan Swallow. Copyright 1958 by Alan Stephens. "Prologue: Moments in a Glade" from *Sequoia.* "Encounters" from *Poetry.* "Be With Me," "Morning Peace," "The Visitor" first appeared in *Genesis West.*

GEORGE P. ELLIOTT: "Blind" first published in *Western Review.* "Five-in-one" from *The Hudson Review.* "His Cataract is Removed Letting the Light In" appeared in *Beloit Poetry Journal.* "Spelunker" from *Stand and Inland.* "Photographer to Lady" from *Perspective.* "When I was a Bird" from *Window and Coastlines.* "Reading Some Materialists" appeared in *Furioso.* "To a Bird" first published in *Poetry.* "In Warm and Strangeing Moonlight" originally published in the *New Republic.* Permission to reprint from the author.

LEONARD NATHAN: "Apologia" first appeared in *The New Republic.* "Man and Wife" from *Epoch.* "Orpheus Again and Again" from *Massachusetts Review.* "To One Who Lost Her Son" appeared in *Poetry.* "Aftermath of a Loss" and "Father and Daughter" from *UCLAN Review.* "Epithalamion" appeared originally in *Discovery.* "Wings" from *The Reconstructionists.*

CONTENTS

PREFACE

The primary aim in making a Talisman Anthology is to offer the reader a collection of good poetry. That aim could have included a multitude of authors and of poems, but was limited at the outset by two considerations: first, that the projected anthology was only to be so long and no longer; and second, that Talisman Press has always been concerned mainly with the western United States. These considerations prompted the editors to look for some rule of thumb for inclusions and exclusions, a rule that would augment the too-liberal one of poetic quality. We came down to the notion that only western poets would be included, although we were careful not to specify too closely what "western" meant, on the principle that the best of faiths begin to crumble under the demands of precise definition. This notion of "western" left us with a card file of what seemed like hundreds of poets more or less well-known and published. The thought of how many poets we had missed was too chilling to dwell on for long. We thought of setting dates, arbitrary ones like "from 1930 to 1955," but this evasion still left us with an unmanageable drawer full of cards. Then, second, third, and fourth thoughts suggested that the representative slice-of-life anthology, wherein hundreds of names cancelled each other, was more a sociological than a literary phe-

13

nomenon. It became clear that if we were going to back off from the worst of the problem, we needed a plain, unanswerably irrational means of making the book we originally envisaged.

The final solution was to give western poets who had published in Talisman Magazine and who had written what we felt were a number of good poems, a clutch of pages in which to have their say. We made one exception in the instance of Howard Baker who had not published in Talisman Magazine, and so we lost the invulnerability of well-meaning unreasonableness. But we felt strongly that Mr. Baker's work, which received deserved attention some years ago, had been lost to readers of poetry and that it should have a hearing again. Mr. Baker is a long-time westerner and a good poet, so our consciences are partly clear. I suppose that we could have made other exceptions, but none occurred to us (they will no doubt occur to others), perhaps because we ran out of allotted space.

A few other, secondary aims are perhaps worth mentioning: We sought to present a variety of styles in the anthology. We hate neither the iambic pentameter nor the "loose" modern line—so long as they both seem to function organically in their kinds of poem. The classical regularity of Alan Stephens and the relaxed accentuals of William Stafford made for a considerable range of technique, just as Mr. Stephens' (if we may take the liberty to label him) rational stoicism and Mr. Stafford's religious humanism (another label for which we beg pardon) show a considerable range of attitude. And within the work of each of these poets, whom we have rather arbitrarily here picked as exemplary poles in the anthology, there is enough variety to render labels happily inapplicable.

Anyway, it is the poetry, not the technique, attitude, or name, that we are offering; it is the poetry that the reader will confront, we hope without too many presuppositions about words like "poetry," "western," "academic," "free," and the rest of the cant of professional and amateur criticism, too often more concerned with its own abstract constructions than with the-thing-itself. The-thing-itself, in many aspects, we now offer and trust that the reader will find in the following what is worthy of his pleasurable attention.

*   *   *   *   *

However well or badly the editors have done their job, it ought to be said here that they owe the opportunity for doing it at all, first, to the poets themselves who have been unexceptionally cooperative; second, to Alan Swallow whose quiet service to poetry never can be enough praised; and third, to Carol Nash who held the whole project together with a typewriter, patience, and her steadying and sympathetic intelligence.

THE EDITORS
TALISMAN PRESS

ANN STANFORD

Ann Stanford is a native of Southern California. She attended Stanford University, where she studied law and was associated with the Stanford group of poets. Her first published appearance was in *Twelve Poets of the Pacific,* edited by Yvor Winters. At the time of her graduation she was awarded the James D. Phelan Fellowship in Literature to work on a projected book-length narrative poem, *Magellan.*

Her first two books of lyric poetry were published by Alan Swallow. They are titled *In Narrow Bound* (1943) and *The White Bird* (1949). In 1957 she received a fellowship to Yaddo, the writers' colony at Saratoga Springs, New York, where she finished *Magellan.* This poem was published by the Talisman Press in 1958 and won first place in the Browning awards given at Redlands University, as well as the Silver Medal for Poetry of the Commonwealth Club of California.

Ann Stanford has been on the staff of the University of California, Los Angeles, as an instructor in Journalism, and has taught the writing of poetry in the Extension Division of that University. She is now an assistant professor of English at San Fernando Valley State College. She is also the staff poetry reviewer for the Los Angeles *Times* and the editor of the *Uclan Review.* Her poem "Pandora" was recently chosen for the first award in the Borestone Mountain Poetry Awards anthology, *Best Poems of 1960.*

Of her own work she says: "I write poetry because it makes me feel good to write it. If what I say strikes a response in the reader, so much the better. I try to describe as exactly what I feel as simply as I can. I am not concerned with style, except as it may be used to reinforce whatever I am trying to get at in the poem."

THE WEATHERCOCK

Wind shakes me
I am weak and spent
With every argument.
I doubt and hang
A breath disturbs me.
Sinewless and vain
The harsh and soft are one to me
Zephyr or gale, I turn my face to it.

North wind and south have whispered
And I go with each.
The dulcet evidence of bloom and spring
Or the cold reason of on-circling storm
Both have convinced me, and I yearn with them
Yearn as the smoke drift or the lifted leaves.

Yet I proportion my stance to the breeze.
Wind shall not take me
Though he shriek and bite
Frighten all other birds to leeward shade
Blow down the pigeons from the cooing lofts
Sail the hawk back downwind and send
Laborious eagles panting to their rocks.

I have set my claw
Deep in the roof's pinnacle,
There to hold
While solid objects knock about—
Each broadside thing—
Stiff in this hub to turn and, keen,
Broach to the wind a practiced waywarding.

Though the barn totters
And hay flies
And the wood is pierced by pebbles;
Till the ties of the timber skew
With the beams ajar
And the shingles scatter
And the great roof falls

I crow though none may hear.
In the vast spinning world, I still point true.
I fly here.

THE WALNUTS

There shine always the bright tops of the grove
And within that forest mysteries of birds,
In the autumn, the clear crackle of leaves
And the walnut pickers. Dark-skirted after them

The gleaners. Trees, trees were everywhere.
Out of the banks of a foggy morning,
Outside the windows, the sweet trees leaned
Tasselled in spring, in holy burst of leaves.

And the oats made meadows of the early year—
With nodes for whistles, the juice sweet and thin—
Grown high to bend into rooms, and yellow flowers
Hung over the spicy tunnels under the trees.

There the grove, hanging forever real in the air.
And I an exile, knowing every turn
And turning home, and lost in the dazzled road
The strange, swept premises, and the great trees gone.

PANDORA

Never, never again the house new or youth precise
Or the fresh loaves of hay in the field.
And the tree bark shimmers black and white
Only after rain.

The day rose clear-faced and quick
Breathing lemon and sage, undoubtedly crystal,
Fog was for coolness, not to get lost in, and the wicked
Rode to ominous music.

The box had been left, but I never suddenly opened the
    lid.
The day hung so full, time being happy and short,
No reason to fret over a dusty chest in a corner,
And I had given my word.

But nothing is changeless. While it was there in the house
Something crept out, buzzing and small.
I heard it at night, an insect whine in the air
Unseen in the light.

And the mornings were sad sometimes
And rising slow, and the day crumpled and worn
Like a picture handled too much,
And I indifferent.

Came haze outlasting the dawn
Between me and the fields, the horizon too close;
And bright days were full of objects
Not noticed before.

Love broke to a trinity, there were too many paths;
None seemed to be true, and in the oat fields the horsemen
Wore various guises, and which could I trust
On their spotted geldings?

I have heard of such things, but not for myself,
And the silver sifts from the box
On my hair and my tears, and the owner is gone, and I—
I shall never be rid of it.

THE GENIE

I dwell
In a dark small cell
Turbulent against walls
Constricting smoke and flame,
Fire, essence, into a coal which glows
And gasps to spread, for the expanding green
Billowing flow of love and the upper air.

Taut in myself
Wound hard, contained in flesh,
Identified, bounded, traced—unknown
I am the blood that echoes in a shell
I roil, the surge of ocean wrapped in shore
I roll, a universe kept in a crystal jar,
I am the muted genie pressed within.

I burst
In seed and passion,
In the white of fire
The hoar of ice. Unfetter me, I cry
And I am spent in tumult before night.
Move, Earth, charred and blackened on the sun
I rise and swell upon such destiny.

Within this verdigris
I twist in torment.
Out, out, or I am buried here,
Lest eons seal my burning into stone—
Quenched into marble, let my age not pass.
Yet pause, hand to the lamp and know
The furious spirit you are letting go.

LOST OBJECTS

Things disappear. The ball that flew
Over the fence and caught in space,
The ring, dropped unnoticed out of view,
Even the strongbox fastened in place.

Things rove while you are gone; they change.
A pair should not be reckoned two,
So common that it is not strange:
One glove, one lover, half, one shoe.

To know the ache of the intensely lost
Think her yours who was her own,
Slipped off without goodnight, poor guest.
Even a statue shifts in its stone.

Motion holds all, the tumblers turn
Through new gyrations in their airy shells
And shunt within till we become
Lost pieces of ourselves.

NOTES TO GO WITH A COMPASS

1.
Straight to the north, if you should go that way,
Are the wet Cascades that wring out the sea
And beyond, the Canadian taiga forest,
Spruce and fir that dwindle north to less

And less; finally the grassy tundra plain.
Birds cluster, and flowers fashion arctic spring
Toward endless noon, earth and shore bountiful.
Land gives way to the sea, a salt so chill

It thickens to a crystal continent.
The compass veers and shivers on its stem.
The bare stars and steady sextant show
How absolute is north upon the pole.

2.
One step will take you south, from absences
Of warmth, wet, green, and all complexities
To slow rains transforming brown to dull
To brighter plains, where foliage, prodigal

Overruns itself. Atlantics on the leaves
Augment the Amazon's gigantic trees.
And earth is hidden in the visible,
The steamy self-grown tangle of Brazil.

3.
Few push such ultimates. This compass, say,
Will help to cross that ridge in a straight line—
No matter how you twist among the trees—
Or brings you through the bareness of a plain.

Or lose the current, or the stars deceive
Here is a truth to move the hesitant
And is what most will use a compass for,
Not trending toward perfection like a saint.

The towns are marked. The road is clear between,
The ruggedness a temporary thing.
This toy helps only him who knows the way
As a bird unfolds direction with the wing.

HIDDEN THINGS

1.
Upon the wall, drawn by a child's hand,
The horses twitch their tails or clash their hooves
In formal duel in an unreal land.
And they are sealed in stillness, though all moves

About them. No one sees them paw the air
For they are painted over, and no stain
Shows where they fly. Yet certainly they are there.
They are secret as the packet sealed with chain

To the courier's wrist, and even more, for none
Shall read what codes this flying herd might bring.
And so they stretch in their impenetrable zone.
Beneath engulfments of ocean, ground, and green

2.
Between the lid of the box and the enclosed
Or the layers of paint or leaf, under sheared surfaces,
The hidden things broaden and are disposed
As rounded bodies in immeasurable space.

As gold beaten to foil may yet endure
Another stroke, and thin and thin again
So does each changing layer yield but more
The wheels and chambers of the finest plane.

No violence attains these inward stores.
Nor the slow fall of stealth, or shifts of day
Complete their rendezvous, although we shower
Echo with roar and labor. Suddenly

We are within the sound that we have made,
Within the box, and mystery surrounds
With vacancies of sun, enclosing shade
Of articulate blue. It is no simple ground

On which we walk, but treasuries of roots
And stones and hollow chambers, and the slow
Descent of parting things. How lonely broods
The orchard, raising the green whispering show

Of summer through the roofs of cottages,
Through lawns and asphalt, in incorrigible tiers,
Remembered seasons, and beyond, in that place,
The waving grass of time's old furniture.

3.
What lies beneath the terrace of flesh, the pale
Secluding forehead, in that weir of past
Illusions or hoped events? I cannot tell:
As one walks in darkness past a house

Suffused with radiance, and the curtains pulled
And curious, waits, discovers there a sum
Of uncovered light and finds within revealed
A shadow passing from the empty room.

But could I go within where dark and gold
Lean close together, hear the voices' tremor,
Still I would be outside each separate world
Illumined by its own conservator.

Alas, poor Psyche, did you think the fire,
The quick uncovering of the lamp would prove
By adding sight, the death of your desire?
You only changed unknown, for loss of, love.

4.

Last night, happy and clear, I saw the dead.
We walked together over a wide lawn,
The living not more real than those dear shades,
And leaving to wake, I said farewell again.

Day world of birdsong, when I woke in light
And resonant morning, could any thought distress
This clear existence, paced by breath and bright
Air in which I move. For surfaces

Are hard, and depth the clean repeating of
The seen. The scene cut through and every leaf the same,
A chord of agate, into which we move,
The immortal hardening of a mortal plane.

Yet in this plain, by every light we sense
We lose as much, slipped back into that bend
Of suffering's waste, unrecollected suns—
Lose, and behold only the figured mind,

The dreamed, annihilable soul, psyche
Beyond the surface of the face, and there
Secretly rest. Where absolute abides
Abide all secret things, in an unbroken care.

PERSON AND PLACE

Bright among all else,
Whom the chariot of morning
Brought here and gilt
With auras, so hung,

Shadow of such spirit
That shadow moves among
These corridors as light
And is flame's reflection.

And source neither the sun
Nor the shadow's golden core,
But out of the black borne
Of the drenched interior

That circles what it will
With baubles of light
And makes of this double
A precious weight

That returns upon itself
As though new-perceived
And mirror and source
Mingle and are confused.

And the sun and I contend,
Enamoured of the vision,
Whether it from that god descended
Or has from this dark sea risen.

AN ANNIVERSARY: A COUNTRY BURIAL

Again December shadowed and gray—
A time to die for one who so loved sun—
Brings unshaped mornings, set behind clouds
And takes remembrance a year away.

And still I ride in hushed December sound
Past fields long gathered, and the stubble thin,
To the iron gates, and turn beside the grass—
The road is gravel then—to the fresh mound.

Odd how the shaft of light for an hour shone
(Though the day was rain before and afterward)
Across the pile of bloom, the orchard rows,
The restlessness of mourners gazing on.

We talked and went away; the flowers there
Tended the air of many afternoons
In an empty place where none but loss shall come
With a greeting whispered, foolish, in the air.

THE RIDERS

We made castles of grass, green halls, enormous stem-
    lined rooms
And sailed in trees.
Close to the backyard fence
We dug a cave.
We never finished it,
But there was plenty of time for moving that last foot or
    two of earth—
It was an eternity till Christmas.

Do you remember the yellow fields
We tusseled through, small mustard petals clinging?
And the hikes on Saturday up to the grove of oaks?
Plenty of time then, and dark came down before we were
    home.
They were out calling and searching.

There was a winter year and a summer year.
The last was for beaches.
Salt wind over the gaudy pier,
And things moved faster.
You on the yellow horse, I on the dun.
One way the sea, the battleship,
The pier, the fishers leaning by the rail,
The ferris wheel,
And turning still
The shoddy mermaid painted on the wall.
Up and down we laughed and caught the rings.
And one was gold for summer.

Then summer was gone, and the horse bunched warm
    ripples
Trotting through orchards down to the practice ring.
His eyes were like suns, when he changed his gait
Faster and faster till the trees blurred and the sky
And the warm beast gathering and springing.
How to get off, how to escape!
At last I fell, but it was no better.

The earth turned under my back
Swift, swift, we turned out of day to night to day again,
Light and shadow from a picket fence.

And the planet whirled on the sun, a swift carousel.

Our heads grow gray, our children laugh in the long
    grasses.

THE BEAR
(from the Grimms)

Rose Red:

We have once more caught
This old humbug, sister.
Here he lies in his shaggy coat
Snug by our cordial fire,
Claiming to be a prince, or a lost Christian in disguise.
There are things of the chrysalis—the butterfly,
Plots that must be hatched, deeds long in doing,
But this is thorough bear, rumpled and earthen.

Snow White:

Remember, sister, other miracles
The pellet seed, bursting to root and leaf,
The hard green bud to rose,
The thought newborn
That pecks at the skull like a rousing chick.
Great things from small,
The pearl from the ooze,
And the radiant soul
Rapt from its prison in a broken spell.

Rose Red:

Snakes drop their skins, but remain serpents still,
And the moth, long harbored in its chrysalis
Flies as a birthright to distorting flame.
Leaves spurt from seed, but only for the season.
No one has charted the sea-track of souls.
Bears sleep in winter caves and wake up bears.

The Bear:

The forest offers honey, hollow logs
Streams fraught with fishes,
Berries on the hills.

Yet here I ponder.
I am no common bear, for I have visions.

I dreamed I was a prince;
I walked in halls
Brilliant with torches.
Underneath this pelt
I feel the hardness of the golden mail.
Can such dissatisfaction offer proof
I am enmeshed in spells too fine to ravel?

Snow White, Rose Red, divert your clumsy wooer.
Some day we meet the dwarf and force the answer.

NIGHTPIECE

Here in this chill half-death
Portending dawn, I wake
And drift in little light
Seeing not forms but breath.

The tongue that leapt to scold
Harrying on the young
Is chidden, and the ache
Of love seeps in with cold.

What can I say to Rest?
Only in stillness move
To draw the comfort close,
And know the largeness pressed

On such a few brief years:
Night-spirit, hovered near—
To be the ultimate
The silencer of fears.

PASTORAL ON THE BACK NINE

The back nine's not so much a place for games
As a cropped meadow where the balls are birds
And birds like balls go skimming,
Speed toward the sky in unexpected turn
Or plummet downward from a mythic screen.
We knew the air had substance, now we learn
It is a crystal from whose myriad panes
A ball can bounce and veer and ricochet.
It is with trees and hedges that we play.
Where in the city is the grass so green
Or made for walking through?
The early dew
Shines it to silver and the broken sheen
Stalks the wet golfer like his tracks on snow.

Slow for the young, whose muscles knot and flare
Slashing at tennis, bursting over waves,
It waits like gentle years for everyman.
Two spirit-saving Pilgrims we come here
Our burdens on our shoulders, and the plan
Defined by hazards. Past the parking row
Shrunk to these fair ways, stream beset and rare,
We find the cosmos sloughed off long ago,
Eden again, where heaven flickers near.

THE POOL

All is reflection.
I saw it in the gaze
Of agate nymphs and passersby
So given to beauty
That its homage moved
Plainer than in the freshest woodland pool.

And thus of legend:
Tales of wit and gold
And deeds are mirror-made
To grow in glass, not flesh,
As show dim stars wrought clear
Enlarged in their magnificent passages.

Listen, diminished Echo,
Who disavowed your praise
Comes back to wish your *glory, glory*
Roll maze to maze
Be heard again, again
Repeat the image that you made of me.

Call out, that worth
Is being coveted,
And seek a virtue in the surfaces
Of eyes and words,
That I forget the heart
Shattered or hollow, lost in purposes,
Secluded deep where no one else may press.

THE FLIGHT

There is something still marvelous about setting forth
High into heaven among clouds, where pride
Speaks to the bulk of mist.   Is it not worth
An angel fall to flow with wind and die?

Or swim with currents, which on mountains write
Passage of waters from the ocean's transom,
Over green rocks that skim in our despite
Brilliant toward the heaven of a tomb?

But here in the High Tower I may mend
Through stone and slate, laid formally and well,
The appearance of the earth, returned to tend
The venture that might go too far to tell.

I have the great lawn, where the maples claim
Their own dominion, and I hold such sky
As in towers broods.   The wasp drops down to name
Slowly the budding of the solid day.

THE FACES

There are acres of dark between the lamp and door
Acres of dark wading into the room
Hours to grope while something black comes down
Or springs like a cougar from the shelf, or runs
Against you in the dark, or softly comes
To touch your hand and leave you without sound.

And the light only pushes away the one
That stood the nearest; none of them are gone.
They are beyond the window where the curtain
Is made of dark. You cannot be sure
Of numbers, and the faces are obscure
And they slip off out of the reach of vision.

They hold on shingles or the roof's tower,
Or waver softly in the simple air.
They are pure night, and night is made of these.
Come, let us walk through all these rings,
Let us take night and go among their crowding
And we shall see them high upon the eaves.

And we shall hear them in the quiet of time
Restless behind us when we try to claim
Only faces of light, and we shall see
The same perspective follows as we turn
Suddenly round to catch the vanishing
Of what was there and is not, and might be.

WILLIAM STAFFORD

William E. (dgar) Stafford was born in Hutchinson, Kansas, January 17, 1914. Most of his school years he spent in Hutchinson, but during high school days the family (parents and a brother and a sister besides William) spent time in Liberal and in Wichita, where the father's work for an oil company took them. The family suffered some stringencies during the depression, when William's various jobs at times helped: carrying papers, gardening, construction work. Both parents read voraciously, and the family inhabited the libraries of the towns where they lived.

After junior college in Garden City and in El Dorado, William attended the University of Kansas, from which he was drafted just short of a Master's degree in 1940. Till 1944 William served in alternative service as a conscientious objector, working in soil conservation in Arkansas, in the U.S. Forest Service in California, and as educational secretary for that part of alternative service administered by the Church of the Brethren from their office in Elgin, Illinois. On release William picked up his M.A. from the University of Kansas, offering as his thesis a book about conscientious objectors, *Down in My Heart,* later published by the Brethren Publishing House.

During the later 1940's William worked for Church World Service, a relief organization, in California, taught high school at Chaffey School in Ontario, California, and finally in 1948 joined the English department at Lewis and Clark College, in Portland, Oregon, where he has continued to teach ever since, with two years off to obtain a Ph.D. from the State University of Iowa and with two years at another interval spent in teaching at Manchester College, in Indiana, and at San Jose State College, in

35

California.

Some of the earliest publication achieved was in *Poetry* magazine in the late 1940's; from that time to the present poems have been appearing in literary magazines and in a few magazines of general circulation. A collection, *West of Your City,* was published by Talisman Press in 1960. A few poems have appeared in anthologies. A second book collection was published by Harper and Brothers in late fall of 1962. A great literary creation has been lurking around William for several years; it hovers just out of reach in the early mornings before the children get up, but it slips away. He expects to find it and bring it in, out of the Oregon mist, some time in the 1960's.

In March, 1963, William was awarded the National Book Award for Poetry.

A VISIT HOME

In my sixties I will buy a hat
and wear it as my father did.
At the corner of Central and Main.

There may be flowers by the courthouse windows
and rich offices where those town-men
cheated him in 1929.

For calculation has exploded —
boom, war, oilwells, and, God!
the slow town-men eyes and blue-serge luck.

But at the door of the library I'll lean my cane
and put my hand on buckshot
books: Dewey, Parrington, Veblen . . .

There will be many things in the slant of my hat
at the corner of Central and Main.

SOME SHADOWS

Neither do I love a cloistered virtue —
it is a cold way to live.
But where I come from withdrawal
is easy to forgive.

When Mother was a girl Indians
shadowed that country, the barren lands.
Mother ran to school winter mornings
with hot potatoes in her hands.

She was like this — foreign, a stranger.
She couldn't hear very well;
the world was all far. (Were the others laughing?
She never could tell.)

Later, though she was frightened,
she loved, like everyone.
A lean man, a cruel, took her.
I am his son.

He was called Hawk by the townpeople,
but was an ordinary man.
He lived by trapping and hunting
wherever the old slough ran.

Our house was always quiet.
Summers the windmill creaked, or a board.
I carried wood, never touching anyone.
Winters the black stove roared.

Forgive me the shadows I cling to, good people,
looking here, quiet, at my own prologue.
Hawks cling the barrens wherever I live.
The world says, "Dog eat dog."

RETURN TO SINGLE-SHOT

People who come back refuse to touch
what has been theirs, and in their speech
they give the words a twist, a foreign sound.
Cautiously they walk, wanting all they find
this time to be something else, for someone else.
Then each comes to a stop before the house
longest his, and in his perfect speech
repeats: "This is my house, and I am
still myself." And that restarts the town.

Their fingers find again the grain of wood;
they memorize the promise of the land:
what curves reliably comes back right;
to a fence, responsibility is not obsolete.
One aims a single-shot and hears the muffled past
interject that old, flat, simple sound —
the name of Daniel Boone's psychiatrist.

CEREMONY

On the third finger of my left hand
under the bank of the Ninnescah
A muskrat whirled and bit to the bone.
The mangled hand made the water red.

That was something the ocean would remember:
I saw me in the current flowing through the land,
rolling, touching roots, the world incarnadined,
and the river richer by a kind of marriage.

While in the woods an owl started quavering
with drops like tears I raised my arm.
Under the bank a muskrat was trembling
with meaning my hand would wear forever.

In that river my blood flowed on.

WALKING WEST

Anyone with quiet pace who
walks a gray road in the West
may hear a badger underground where
in deep flint another time is

Caught by flint and held forever,
the quiet pace of God stopped still.
Anyone who listens walks on
time that dogs him single file,

To mountains that are far from people,
the face of the land gone gray like flint.
Badgers dig their little lives there,
quiet-paced the land lies gaunt,

The railroad dies by a yellow depot,
town falls away toward a muddy creek.
Badger-gray the sod goes under
a river of wind, a hawk on a stick.

A DIARY ENTRY

The State has taught its men a new kind of organized
quickness in death, more than Achilles knew
about war. Aimed like a gun at certain parts
of the world, they must be ready at night to kill
anyone, even the treacherous equal called friend,
    and launch the end.

I walk this fall a dusty road, alien
to all but what is immediate, ready like other
wanderers to meet some one, to sing, to be
in love. To Hell with the State!
But I am touched by a certain oldfashioned regret:

No way to give anyone the round weight of this day,
the sing of the sun, the plumage of the field
all turned into one ready bird while the year departs —
a man who deserved all this was killed today.
I feel a certain debt to pay — and now no way.

A DOCUMENTARY FROM AMERICA

When the Presidential candidate came to our town
he had used up his voice, but he delivered a speech
written by a committee, through a friend of his
running on the same ticket. The candidate smiled.
We cheered his courage, and a cynic hissed:
"Fools, you are on TV and have just helped elect that
        man!"

Later at a motel in Nanton, Alberta,
(a town on the plains with a special surprise —
a pipe that gushes a drink like a flash by the road)
we tuned in a show with a variety of plots
to stalk viewers with (whereas Westerns had only
to open up with one, say a .44), there in the twilight.

In the midst of a commercial we had democratically
elected and now found delivered forever on the screen,
we were interrupted to learn we had just won a war,
certified by experts to be correct. We felt at ease:
conscience a subliminal bonus, delivered
by flags and that eerie music when the enemy appeared.

Then there was our candidate smiling at our crowd,
just as an interviewer invaded our motel to ask what
        program
we were watching. "Oh God," we said, "we were watching
us, watching us." And in a terrible voice he roared,
"Quick, be smiling; you are on the air again!" and —
a terrrible thing—we said just as he said, "How do
        you do."

BOOM TOWN

Into any sound important
a snake puts out its tongue;
so at the edge of my home town
every snake listened.

And all night those oil well engines
went talking into the dark;
every beat fell through a snake,
quivering to the end.

This summer, home on a visit,
I walked out late one night;
only one hesitant pump, distant,
was remembering the past.

Often it faltered for breath
to prove how late it was;
the snakes, forgetting away through the grass,
had all closed their slim mouths.

THAT EARLY SPRING

When blizzards fought the redbud down,
I walked through petals mixed with snow.
There was a tunnel where I walked.
And even now I know which way to go

To find that north. With native coin
still held in my native hand,
when redbud comes too early, I
walk late blizzards in this foreign land.

THE HERO LEARNING TO LEAVE HOME

Ordered by straight sounds
that laced through the house along its morning,
the boy went following what he could find:

The bat in the mulberry tree,
brown-curled like a leaf, upside down,
a part of the night sky held still all day;

The chokecherry thicket, writhing
and promising only its own way, a tangle
richer than the family's whole lifetime.

Meeting them later, the boy's face
included everyone's earlier stare:
"Beyond this place is many another place,

Called *Everywhere*."

CONNECTIONS

Ours is a low, curst, under-swamp land
the raccoon puts his hand in,
gazing through his mask for tendrils
that will hold it all together.

No touch can find that thread, it is too small.
Sometimes we think we learn its course —
through evidence no court allows
a sneeze may glimpse us Paradise.

But ways without a surface we can find
flash through the mask only by surprise —
a touch of mud, a raccoon smile.

And if we purify the pond, the lilies die.

AT THE SALT MARSH

Those teal with traveling wings
had done nothing to us but they were meat
and we waited for them with killer guns
in the blind deceitful in the rain.

They flew so arrowy till when they fell
where the dead grass bent flat and wet
that I looked for something after nightfall
to come tell me why it was all right.

I touched the soft head with eyes gone
and felt through the feathers all the dark
while we steamed our socks by the fire
and stubborn flame licked the bark.

Still I wonder, out through the raw blow
out over the rain that levels the reeds,
how broken parts can be wrong but true.
I scatter my asking. I hold the duck head.

ICE-FISHING

Not thinking other than how the hand works
I wait until dark here on the cold
world rind, ice-curved over simplest rock,
where the tugged river flows over hidden
springs too insidious to be quite forgotten.

When the night comes I plunge my hand
where the string of fish know their share
of the minimum. Then, bringing back my hand
is a great sunburst event; and slow
home with me over unmarked snow

In the wild flipping warmth of won-back thought
my boots, my hat, my body go.

WEATHER REPORT

Light wind at Grand Prairie, drifting snow.
Low at Vermilion, forty degrees of frost.
Lost in the Barrens, hunting over spines of ice,
the great sled dog Shadow is running for his life.

All who hear — in your wide horizon of thought
caught in this cold, the world all going gray —
pray for the frozen dead at Yellow Knife.
These words we send are becoming parts of their night.

HAIL MARY

Cedars darkened their slow way
over the gravel in town graveyards
in places we lived — Wichita, or Haven.

By themselves, withdrawn, secret little shadows
in their corners by the iron gate,
they bowed to the wind that noticed them,

Branches bending to touch the earth;
or night raised them to block the sun
with a thousand utterly weak little hands,

Reciting. They say candle-vigilant woods
in high Arizona swirl twisting upward
out of red dust miles of such emphasis,

Like them, dark by dark by dark.

LEVEL LIGHT

Sometimes the light when evening fails
stains all haystacked country and hills,
runs the cornrows and clasps the barn
with that kind of color escaped from corn
that brings to autumn the winter word —
a level shaft that tells the world:

It is too late now for earlier ways;
now there are only some other ways,
and only one way to find them—fail.

In one stride night then takes the hill.

GLIMPSES

By a simple bridge, a log, we cross;
by a simple river, drink. We take
an oar, push off; pile with rock our briefcase
full of plans, and watch it sink.
It is a simple river.

We climb a cliff, turn right, peer down; sea lions
drag their bulks along wave-battered streets,
charge in armor fat, caught by tide,
their chests enforced by other tide, by anger.
Flippers atilt, they drag.

By distancing that sight, enhanced, we peer
far into other selves — through hate, through tide:
all creatures graced and caught by forming seas
Confront our simple need — to find the world,
reach far, but still to Be.

A RITUAL TO READ TO EACH OTHER

If you don't know the kind of person I am
and I don't know the kind of person you are
a pattern that others made may prevail in the world
and following the wrong god home we may miss our star.

For there is many a small betrayal in the mind,
a shrug that lets the fragile sequence break
sending with shouts the horrible errors of childhood
storming out to play through the broken dyke.

And as elephants parade holding each elephant's tail,
but if one wanders the circus won't find the park,
I call it cruel and maybe the root of all cruelty
to know what occurs but not recognize the fact.

And so I appeal to a voice, to something shadowy,
a remote important region in all who talk:
though we could fool each other, we should consider —
lest the parade of our mutual life get lost in the dark.

For it is important that awake people be awake,
or a breaking line may discourage them back to sleep;
the signals we give — yes or no, or maybe —
should be clear: the darkness around us is deep.

ONE DAY IN AUGUST

There in the suddenly
  still
    wide street lay
Spot.

No dog so alone
  should
    ever have to mean
That—

Suddenly forever
  Still.

TRUTH IS THE ONLY WAY HOME

A few that I've known knew I had to talk to them,
that the only way on was what we were saying;

Most have looked over my shoulder for the next man,
thinking what to say if, when — somewhere else.

Whatever was calling them, it doesn't matter now:
they were part of some purpose I contended with, and lost.

But just as there are certain remote-nesting birds
cutting little known sky for the straight way home,

So in my life a few arctic terns
are on the course I follow in just the right wind.

Continents turn summer wherever we fly;
the future leans to take our shadows.

ONE HOME

Mine was a Midwest home — you can keep your world.
Plain black hats rode the thoughts that made our code.
We sang hymns in the house; the roof was near God.

The light bulb that hung in the pantry made a wan light,
but we could read by it the names of preserves —
outside, the buffalo grass, and the wind in the night.

A wildcat sprang at Grandpa on the Fourth of July
when he was cutting plum bushes for fuel,
before Indians pulled the West over the edge of the sky.

To anyone who looked at us we said, "My friend";
liking the cut of a thought, we could say "Hello."
(But plain black hats rode the thoughts that made our
    code.)

The sun was over our town; it was like a blade.
Kicking cottonwood leaves we ran toward storms.
Wherever we looked the land would hold us up.

THE FARM ON THE GREAT PLAINS

A telephone line goes cold;
birds tread it wherever it goes.
A farm back of a great plain
tugs an end of the line.

I call that farm every year,
ringing it, listening, still;
no one is home at the farm,
the line gives only a hum.

Some year I will ring the line
on a night at last the right one,
and with an eye tapered for braille
from the phone on the wall

I will see the tenant who waits —
the last one left at the place;
through the dark my braille eye
will lovingly touch his face.

"Hello, is Mother at home?"
No one is home today.
"But Father — he should be there."
No one - no one is here.

"But you — are you the one . . . ?"
Then the line will be gone
because both ends will be home:
no space, no birds, no farm.

My self will be the plain,
wise as winter is gray,
pure as cold posts go
pacing toward what I know.

IN DEAR DETAIL, BY IDEAL LIGHT

1.
Night huddled our town,
plunged from the sky.
You moved away.
I save what I can of the time.

In other towns, calling my name,
home people hale me, dazed;
those moments we hold,
reciting in the evening,

Reciting about you, receding
through the huddle of any new town.
Can we rescue the light
that happened, and keeps on happening, around us?

Gradually we left you there
surrounded by the river curve
and the held-out arms,
elms under the streetlight.

These vision emergencies come
wherever we go—
blind home
coming near at unlikely places.

2.
One's duty: to find a place
that grows from his part of the world—
it means leaving
certain good people.

Think: near High Trail, Colorado,
a wire follows cottonwoods
helping one to know—
like a way on trust.

That lonely strand leaves the road
depending on limbs or little poles,
and slants away,
hunting a ranch in the hills.

There, for the rest of the years,
by not going there, a person could believe
some porch looking south,
and steady in the shade—maybe you,

Rescued by how the hills
happened to arrive where they are,
depending on that wire
going to an imagined place

Where finally the way the world feels
really means how things are,
in dear detail,
by ideal light all around us.

HOWARD BAKER

The idea of an autobiography makes me feel hopelessly heavy-handed. However. I was born in 1905, on April 5, which for some fairly pointless reasons I like to remember was Thomas Hobbes's birthday. I started studying Renaissance manifestations at Stanford in 1927, continued it in Paris and in Berkeley (Ph.D., U.C., 1937).

In Paris I wrote poetry and a novel, *Orange Valley*, 1931. While living in Paris I was befriended beyond measure — personally and as a writer — by Ford Madox Ford. Earlier I had benefited by the help of Yvor Winters in my attempts to write poetry.

I taught at Harvard 1937 to 1943. Then I came to California to write. I have no Georgics to show for that, but possibly I've lived them. Like Sterne, I've planted a tree (too many trees), begotten a child (one more than one), and written. I've been on a school board, acted in a community theater, and worked in farmers' cooperatives. I did another year of teaching, at Berkeley 1958-59, which in certain ways resembled a pleasant visit among old friends rather than a return to an occupation.

My wife, Dorothy Baker, is a much better writer than I am. Prose writer, I mean; she has never tried poetry. But she has her troubles too, mainly structural troubles; so we have collaborated. One joint venture turned out especially well — a television play for Playhouse 90 called the *Ninth Day*. It's about the future and the stubborn unquenchable hopes of human beings.

Lately I have been working with Renaissance philosophy, seeking to get hold of its underlying scepticism, to which I believe we must all return now and begin building anew, this time more existentially than in the past. It might be a book someday.

ODE TO THE SEA

O first created and creating source,
Beloved rib of elemental force;
   Being, in whose deep thighs
   Nascence remotely lies,
Whose golden arms still dripping of the stream
And liquid eyes inform my deepest dream —
   Spotless daughter of Time,
   Teach me his paradigm!
Patient and perfect literate, say how
I may conciliate the Then and Now!

What is the Now? Is it my present glance
Drifting upon this shaken blue expanse?
   The showering sun upon my face,
   My breath inhaling salty space?

Time seems to focus on this lonely beach;
It crowds my taste and sight, and pours the speech
   Of living Sea into my ear
   So that naught is, but what I hear:

Behind me but a silent mesa land
Recessive from this fragrant step of sand,
   Only the shelving gulf before,
   Lifting a low deep-structured roar.

Yet listen, for that crumbling sound is one
With the long roll of winds behind the sun;
   And vision, freed, may mark
   This glow-worm Earth in dark
Lowlands of space, or moving closer see
Our globe beclouded like an April tree
   With green beneath the spray:

There, on the green and gray
Danubian plains, our race made dusky stage:
There sleeps pale Crete, there northern forges **rage.**

The present time is not so small nor dense
That it lies here incompassed by my sense;
   And past and future times are naught
   But modes of individual thought.

Pondering this, I watch the balanced sea —
How from the surf the smooth blue arches flee
   Out, out upon the globe's cold side
   Where purest magnitudes abide,

Where time, eventless, melts away, and then
Grows absolute, devoid of deeds of men!
   Devoid of pride, of shame and crime,
   And time itself devoid of time!

Deep hollow Sea, I am but human kind!
Your sloping azure dales dismay my mind;
   I see your mantle swirled
   Along an empty world
Beckoning where I cannot come, and live.
And live! Ask, Sea, no more than I can give!
   Love with the lover dies;
   With drowned and bleaching thighs,
Clutching your gift of seaweed in my hand,
I should return still undissolved to land!

Man lives with shadeless meadows at his side;
He reckons that his earthly deeds provide
   Fruits for a shading temporal vine,
   Gourds for the well, cool, green, and fine;

The shaggy vine in multiplicity
Matches the pale perfections of the sea,
   But the clear modes of Sea prevail
   Over the vine's complex detail:

Up from the bright sea-coasts our history twines
Sensitive, frail, — uncared for, it declines.
   We know the grip of long sea-hours,
   But count our days by drouths and showers.

In modes of specious presentness, what store,
O Sea, of past events, endows this shore?
   What was the quick gaunt ring
   Of voices by the spring?
And what the silent gazing wonderment
Of eyes on nameless tree and creature bent?
   Where wept the old grandee
   Recurrent harms of Sea?
And where emerged from waves upon these sands
That priest who carried God in drenchèd hands?

Fragments!—From fragments history here descends
Upon a bare mud house where seaward bends
   A river-bed. The folk are poor,
   The mesa silent as the spoor

Of the coyote. Mongrels hold the wall
For shade, and roam by night. Prayers recall
   Stanchioning names to tongues inside —
   Names like the ruined spars the tide

Casts up, the craft's homeport and tons unknown.
Sometimes the folk, when dry east winds have blown,
   Stooping for shells along the beach,
   With sea-roar blend a bird-like speech.

Evenings with desert glooms enclose their days.
Westward each night the sea's low radiance strays
  Into a brilliant sky.
  So institutions die.
Conserving Sea! To what auroral plains
Have you consigned the meaning of the names
  Augustine, Abelard,
  Aquinas, Bede, Bernard?
Permanent, lossless, undiminished Sea,
Change is the law of your stability!

Swift from the sea comes change; and Christendom—
Like childhood gardens echoing the hum
  Of words from the parental lip —
  Vanishes with the rising ship.

The liner slanting southward changes place
Mysteriously, as if both sea and space,
  Under compulsions of its will,
  Retreat from it while it stands still:

It rends perspectives, it commands the Now!
I with the sea's low eyes inspect its bow,
  Its funnels, inset decks and bridge,
  Steadily from my splashëd ridge.

How well I know the structures of my age!
This long, compact, careering ship is gauge
  And archetype of them all:
  Here man's import is small
Beside the turbine, his rewards are slight;
And yet for some the engines spin delight.
  The ship has rich cuisine,
  Damasks of frosty sheen,
Flowers and wine, with music brass and bold;
And tools, to flay the heathen, in the hold.

Wreathed with horizons momentarily green,
Drunk as a caesar who has lately seen
    Auspice in birds' fastidious flight,
    The ship assails the casual night.

Think that this Leviathan of Ocean,
This dense projection of incarnate motion,
    Moves only under someone's hand,
    Labors, and answers his command;

Whatever weaker nations it offends,
However it disrupts their codes for ends
    Potentially both good and ill,
    It shapes the world to someone's will.

Men and not monsters warp the bounds of Sea.
Yet may not thoughtless men still monsters be?
    Not fate but men unlock
    The energies of rock,
And to what ends? O guileful Sea, they ask
Only in your false presentness to bask,
    And recklessly to throw
    Their navies on those slow
Confounding graveyards, where dank weeds enchain
The junks of China and the fleets of Spain!

Nations, as thoughtless as Narcissus, drown
Amidst their shattered triumph, and go down
    Gasping a pledge still to restore
    What time has riven from their shore!

I, on my coppery beach, regret the falls,
Not of their banners, but their sober halls.
    — And suddenly there blows on me
    The sterner discipline of Sea:

History is long. Nor men nor nations bear
Lasting degrees of value. They who stare
   Backwards see but themselves impure.
   Man is collective. Change is sure.

The surf is brushing at my steps; I seek
An aged cliff that stands among the sleek
   Young chargers of the sea.
   Bounds of anemone
And areas by sea-urchins held, devise
The narrow range in which the tides will rise
   And fall, though cliffs themselves
   And all the earth's vast shelves
Crumble. And there the mode of permanence
Is fram'd in the sea-tide's changeful cadence.

Sibilant, whispering Sea, beyond the steep
And thorny reach of doubt, your peace hangs deep;
   In its abundant room
   One views the ways of doom
And, viewing, may withhold the part of fear.
O steady in your variance, appear
   Unceasing in my eye,
   And let me now descry
My course, for I return to inland ground
Burdened, yet to the nascent future bound!

THE OLD ACTOR AND HIS CONSCIENCE

Pay me my rent, Agamemnon,
Pay me my rent for your shoes,
Agamemnon.

Nonsense. My shoes are bought and paid for.

Look at your shoes,
Agamemnon.
Have you ever
Paid me rent for them?

These shoes, my friend?
They're company shoes. Properties.

Don't try quibbling with me,
Agamemnon.
I want rent.

I know nothing of virtue. Therefore nothing
Of debts, obligations . . .

Rent, rent,
Agamemnon!
What's a classic?

Leave me in peace, old man.
There's still another scene to play.

Do those buskins
You strut so noticeably in
Make a classic?

No, not the buskins. Not the decor . . .

What then?

Not the isolated vices. Not
Lechery nor
Chicanery nor
Political outrage nor . . .

Come, come, I want none of your tricks.

A classic does not shun the vicious the
Depraved the
Violent.
In tragedy vice is
Multiform, leaving small way out.
In tragedy, all's composite passion
Wherein evils only
Offset one another.

Is this honest coin you give me?

It's my small inheritance. That,
And this: Virtue, it may be,
Consists in the opposite
Of fanaticism. The opposite, too,
Of sensual predilection.
Virtue consists in playing
The play through. All of it. Both
In its breadth and its length. Which now,
With your permission, I must do.

Rent, Agamemnon!
What of Demos?
What of the gods?

After the show, old man. After the show.

THE FALL OF MILETUS: 494 B.C.

Last night Miletus lost a wall,
And on our ramparts with the dawn
The Persians swarmed like tulips, tall,
Bright-turbaned, long-armed . . . looking down,
Poised to destroy our dusty town . . .

(Already, had they known, Miletus was their own.)

Birth by the sea, death by the sea!
The island cities lent us ships,
And fleet dared fleet momentously;
Till sapped by heat and Persian wiles,
Tiremes turned back toward homeward isles.

(We fell at Mycale, on rostrums by the sea.)

"The twelve Ionian cities are,"
Said Thales, "like a faulty jar
Without a center under stress.
We must agree upon a center."
So each laid claim to centralness.

(We fell at Branchidae, at templed Didymi.)

Though bought and sold, nor love nor gold
Translates the wands and fruited pods
And gloomy splendors of the gods.
Too near, too far! Their ancient glory

Pales into marble allegory.

Tell this in Athens, tell
How their Miletus fell.

But tell this too: that in these motes
Of casual dancing dust, we've seen
The very keel under the sheen
Of things: this casual dancing dust connotes
The pattern hurled upon the world,
And though this city's gone
Its death lives on and on.

PONT NEUF

Henry the Fourth rides in bronze,
His shoulders curved and pensive, thrust
Enormously into electric
Blazonments of a Christmas trust.

Children pass him, aghast and pleased,
Reflective of the flickerings
Of jerky bears and clowns. Alone,
Astute to all the bickerings

Of age and death rides Henry the Grand.
A lean tug shudders in the Seine;
And Notre Dame is black, a relic
Of the blood of other men.

Peace to the other men! And peace
To the mind that has no century,
And sees the Savage pull the statue down,
And down the bear and clown!

CLINTON WILLIAMS

Otho Clinton Williams, Jr. born May 17, 1908 in Fort Worth, Texas. Boyhood in Oklahoma City, Oklahoma. Youth in Los Angeles, California, while it was still a growing city surrounded by towns. A banker-father led to part time jobs in banks. A.B. in 1930 from U.C.L.A., and in 1935, a fugitive from a Burrough's bookkeeping machine and a teller's window, an M.A. from U.S.C. To escape from teaching in the 6th and 7th grades and married to a wife who helped immeasurably by going to work, migrated to U.C. at Berkeley in 1936 for more graduate work. Teaching in high school and junior college in Auburn, California, from 1940 to 1943. To Reed College, Portland, Oregon, in 1943 for six months of teaching until I was drafted into U.S. Navy. In the winter of 1944-45 as a petty officer in personnel stationed at the Navy Electrical School at Purdue University on the banks of the Wabash with time on my hands, an office, stationery, and the University Library, I began again to read contemporary poetry. Thought: "I can do better than this." I tried and blush to remember. Encouragement from friends — especially Roberta Holloway and C. F. MacIntyre — helped. Finally seven poems accepted by *Poetry* (Chicago) in 1945 furnished the impetus to keep me writing. And little magazines have kicked me along. Alan Swallow helped with a slender volume *The Optick Glass* in 1952. Back to Reed College briefly after the war in 1946; then to San Jose State College where, having completed the Ph.D. at U.C. in 1950, I am a professor of English and coordinator of the Humanities Program and where, when I can, I still try to formulate something meaningful in verse.

63

EPISTLE FOR MY SON

Trucks, trains, and planes exist; the guns
you pop reverberate against the sun;
no morning cock your equal crows
in sheer delight before the clock. Defy
augury this day you must and fund
tomorrow by disaster missed. Know
the circle charmed where you suppose
yourself omnipotent and wise.

Time now both stops and runs, the clock your calendar,
noon your season. Waking you travel far,
sleeping is real, dreamless is reason.
Daylight peopled is your haunted house;
the spectres ride at night upon my ceiling.
Each father words his nightmares quite unheard
and sleepless lies abed to sweat them out;
these shadows are but shadows to your seeing.

When pearl and coral rich and strange I am
within the sea-change of your mind and time,
yourself no longer both pursuer and pursued,
no longer timeless in the hourly round,
your doom will be, I trust, as mine
the terror of the sure pursuit,
the bitter knowledge that is cordial fruit
to love at midnight in your sleeping house.

I could not wish you less. The perilous
rides lightly now upon your wooden point.
You joust with solid air and deal mock wounds,
no villain other than yourself need be.
Let time permit you voyage into other flesh,
temper your confidence but never cure.
The luxury of unselfish fear be yours,
and known the limits of immortality.

If anything, I would bequeath the strength,
the chance to test it, and the iron length
to father forth your wishes for your son;
not only five blind senses without mind,
not merely bagatelle of happiness.
Life should not end before it has begun,
and terror has its equilibrium.
Other testament would be unkind.

THE INCORRUPTIBLES

Stained stone or mildewed bronze, they stand
beneath an overarch of sky
in countless city-squares, remind
the many of the few who die.

Remind the neon clocks that sand
trickles at a steady rate
between the fingers, flesh or glass,
never quite articulate.

Remind blind flux and grind of cars
that green yet flashes after red,
and hurry fails to overtake
the impervious dead.

Remind the cash-and-carry crowds
that credit is new-minted by
iconoclasts in stone or bronze
to seeing eyes.

These incorruptible in stone
alive denied the pieties
of clocks, cars, crowds. Dead, they atone —
unheeded deities.

VIGNETTE

Somewhere in the history of thought between
Homer hacking at his blunted quill
and Aldous Huxley throwing away his spectacles
she stands astraddle
with those long and slender legs
nude as the eyeball with the lid withdrawn
and holds the swan's white neck between her hands.
The moment's fixed.
Sharp and obscene in the long centuries of lesser facts
the pastoral beauty of the after-act contrives
its memory in mind and sight.
No other immortality achieves
such clarity of wonder and surprise.

POULENC'S *CARMELITES*

Suffer the little foxes to come into us
Gnawing our liver and our lights
That we may know the final ecstasy
Sharp-toothed of sacrifice.

Vixen victim be naivete
That we may know the bitter-sweet
Of virtue meetly lost and paradox
Of apples tart to taste.

Suffer the mind's sharp edge sheer off a skull.
The Goddess wears no worse for it.
Reason, defined however, light or liver,
Stubbornly persists.

two friends

one spins his cocoon of the familiar
and warms himself
rising regularly his bowels move on schedule
he creates himself by repetition
moves in iambic pentameter
sprung into the strange
like Sisyphus agonizing up his endless hill
he does it all over again
is comfortable again

the other chafes at the habitual
feels himself constricted by the known
custom-made
his time and place he discards
after a single wearing
when he can
is certain he will discover eventually
ultimate nakedness
certain a truer light somewhere burns
to illuminate the essential eye
some deeper darkness to reflect it by
each thinks the other quite absurd
I
fictive third
mere name to mediate between absurdities
affection both

STATEMENT

I have been trying for these seven years
to make a verse as simple as a line
shot at a proper angle through a sphere.
Some might discern and care,

say he found and fixed in space and place
a point to measure motion by. His death
is unimportant. So his life. One asks
exactitude of grace.

One might, of course, pretend it's pointless to
attempt standing an egg upon its end.
Such balancing occurs at times, it's true,
and many another feud.

Recalcitrance is almost principle
to steer by if one aims at setting marks
to separate the unfulfilled from full
in any canticle.

Another, calling upon the holy fire,
hammered brass to golden artifact
to sing more surely by than any star
in groping through the dark.

But sun-strike just athwart a crystal sphere,
or old stick thrust across an iron hoop,
the singing school will not disband this year
even if this arrow pierce.

THE MYTHS OF TRUTH: III

Each is someone's centennial year. Applaud
The empty platitudes that drip by drip
As oil upon the troubled ear defraud
Uneasy senses with their counterfeit.
Public speech is suspect: hollow sound
Expounded by the microphone, parlayed
Coaxially into the brain, profound
With echoes of the ripe and rich cliche.
The ritual of centuries collects
In solemn certainties of gown and hood;
The scholar in absentia inspects
Debris at random in the verbal flood
And, drowsy, wonders at the celebration —
Breached in the honor — of cerebration.

THE MYTHS OF TRUTH: VI

Brave to build an island and dwell there,
Habiting trees, rocks, caves by the sung waves,
Peopling green land and sandy shore from mire
And blood refined to air. So many names
Acquire a solid luster in such fire,
Keep brightly when closer colors shade, —
Gold artifacts of envy, love, and ire
Formed and fixed by thought-tormented flame.

Roberts, Edgell, Gordon, Goddard, Brandt,
And other names spelled of mire and blood
People this time, dubitably await
Waves flung upon the sands, the sounding floods
To tell them into that eternity
Of charted islands in an unknown sea.

SEASON PIECE: 1960

Now is an hour for magic. But words
no longer potion our desire. Fall
of syllables upon the ear disturbs
no ghost, evokes no sorcerer to spell
taut wordless ecstasies in blood and nerve.
Pitched to dry rattle of his wooden bells,
medicine of measured dung and curd
has lost its potency to please, appall.
Stomached symbols leave us yet unstirred;
curious we try old rituals,
come at last to simples and to herbs
(despairing of these withered genitals),
and deprecate that poetry we pay
for this salt prose of wisdom and our age.

MYRON BROOMELL

Myron H. Broomell writes his autobiography as follows — perhaps mostly between the lines:

"I was born in Boston, and — as it happened — on the ninety-ninth anniversary of the birth of the poet Longfellow, of whom I feel myself to be in some respects a coëval.

"Between 1912 and 1956 I had some formal education, but I think I can be described as largely self-educated, if at all, although I should certainly credit my mother with teaching me the three R's and the system of musical notation.

"I have been getting poems published occasionally for about a third of a century, and even in the period when rhyme was less fashionable than it has rebecome.

"Since 1930 I have had the good fortune to be steadily employed, and I have saved up nearly six months' earnings to provide for my old age, if I have one.

"When I was a teacher I thought as a teacher, but now that I have become a sort of accountant I am sustained by my philosophy: Follow the path of least resistance, and try to keep going."

Mr. Broomell lives in Durango, Colorado.

71

THE TEMPORALITIES

In the mountains the houses neither age nor die.
The paint, the wood, are neither new nor old.
White is not brilliant against winter sky
Nor moss-green loud against a tree in gold.
Nor are they shabby, either, where wind washes
The bone-dry clapboards and the flaking sashes.

As I came around the corner of one such,
Suddenly that was where there is no time.
It had tough grass in the dooryard, but not much,
And one thin vine that would not die nor climb.
With a slight breathing I could outlive the brave
Or say Hi! to my grandsire forty years in his grave.

FOUR SONNETS

AFTER HARVEST

Since at some time the fleshly sensations fade,
The kiss is gone before its lasting message.
The humble body, when the load is weighed,
Is soon unyoked. Meanwhile the heart pays pesage.
The toll was heavy — for the grain was much,
The wain laborious and not quickly come by;
The weigher balanced with a clumsy touch,
The chafferer was new and bargained dumbly.
And since the business rankles, the man frets
Still when the beast is stalled, the grain unladen;
He mumbles prices and laments the weevil.
But sleep at length is restful; he forgets.
So I keep only of a once live maiden
A faint impression of contemptible evil.

OF JUDGMENT

I would not call you light; you are not that,
Who weigh too heavy in the scale of shame;
Nor empty, who held much to shudder at
After one learned to call it by its name;
Nor can I call you vicious, to whom vice
Was virtue's fellow — a bird and another bird
Heard chirp in twilight by an ear not nice.
There ought to be some quainter, juster word.
There ought to be some touch of pity in it,
Some true admission of how fair you seemed
In the irrevocable, age-long minute
Before you grew so wholly disesteemed.
It should confess, this word I do not find,
How hungry you once found me, and how blind.

THE PLEADERS

When we are come to judgment, you and I,
The one to answer for a fault unconscious,
The other for still summoning what is by;
When you have offered the plea unpretentious,
And I have claimed my specious constancy
And set it up against your simple caption
That makes an ordinary jape of me
For raveling an elaborate corruption:
In that hard cause, whose trial might consume
Time out of mind and not be well decided,
I shall appeal to nuance and perfume;
You will recite *It could not be avoided.*
Pleading in different tongues, each will aver
Betrayal by an erring interpreter.

IN STORE

The rendezvous you think you will not keep
Is not with death nor ruin. These you know
May any day surprise you in your sleep,
Or startle the wide eye with a tableau.
Nor do you think forever to avoid
The traveler age, with whom we all fall in —
With whose society Cato was not annoyed,
And whose approval Paris could not win.
The meeting that you reckon to escape
Is less condign than any one of these;
Yet it might give them odds on its strange shape
And the swift way that it could banish ease:
I mean the encounter, dread as with an elf,
When one day you shall turn and see yourself.

WE MUST WRITE OFTEN

Little by little everything fades out—
First the expression of the vivid face,
And then the light that lay behind the eyes.
The mouth, its contours, longer resist doubt,
But then are gone, and only in their place
Something not memory, that them belies.
Afterward all that keeps the image quick
Is the vague trait of carriage through a room—
The way the body leaned, the carmine stick
Lifted against the lips, the one perfume
Was stippled there and there, and then the shoulder
Leaned to the cloak. In those days one was bolder—
Eye being bright with love and little sleep,
The occasion tense, the moment snatched from fate,
The face a flower arranged that might not keep,
The errand urgent and the danger great:
And always there was wine still in the glass,

And kisses not yet tried, and other drink;
And sometimes war excited every heart.
Now it fades out: the flavor of the brass,
The sound of scent, the feeling when you think,
The color of the body's conscious art.

LINES FOR PONCE DE LEON

I.

How shall we love, who in our minds recall
When flesh was God but all the leaves must fall?
For we look back and yearn upon the young,
While they are deaf to any golden tongue.

The young shall never see in the gray hair,
Contemporaneous, what times were there.

Ageless at forty, as at eighty fade
The virgin kiss and the approaching spade,
The lovers of their past in thought behold
Each ravished hope bestowing happy gold —

There glows the youth unscrupulously strong,
And the cool maid his burning length along.

Then, when in retrospect or in their dreams
The old grow young, the young grow real as day,
Almost the moment its exemplar seems;
But now they lack the will and want the way.

Knowing so well what it was like to live,
They still would have what now no death can give.

II.

Since in the shapes of memory no love
Survives except as touching mind and heart,
Because the member in its human glove
Lasts but a moment and forgets the part;

Or since the man whose appetite was sound
Hungers no more when death by famine nears;
And the lost music of the constant round
Ceases when ocean dances in his ears;

Or, lastly, since, from war by time withdrawn,
The peaceful soldier dotes on noble foes,
Counting what generals crimsoned a green lawn
To make him wear the medal history knows;

And all the wounds are weary only when
The maggot still in raw flesh weaves and thrives,
But those who live are the surviving men,
And the hurt brain feels normal all their lives:

Therefore, my love, and you who for me fought,
Forget the cost — for thus I prove it nought.

Yet once suppose the past came sudden back —
The bed in the bright garret now resumed
Its stolen burden, and the jungle track
Teemed as before with all the strong and doomed:

Might those young ghosts their violent hours unfold,
Still could I not, who even then was old.

III.

In former days when man would sleep with woman,
Memorable forever was the intoxication thereof —
The boy's imagination learning to be human,
The man's wishes at home with the body of love.

As we grow older every story seems
To become a legend. There are many that we know,
And all useful in the interpretation of dreams.
The hunchback stranger, the lantern in the falling snow,

The destinable aisles of the forest — all now conspire
As if toward refuge, when no more the warm
Hope of good health shall stand to us as fire,
Nor the body as shelter in the natural storm.

Now you will say to yourself, "Quick, quick! Find the
        answer
Before the clock changes, the shadow sweeping
Over the meadow is gone like a wicked dancer,
Or an old man bent double with recollection
Is found wandering in the market, snuffling and weeping."

But there is no answer; only your own reflection.

From *The City Built on Sand*: No. 5

In the dead noontide when the fog had lifted,
The doors being closed, the gears being all in mesh,
I ran for the bus. The driver had once shifted,
But for a moment we were of one flesh.
Because my garb was fine and his was not,
Because I smiled though panting as I ran,
He let me in and we forsook that spot —
I as a fare and he a kind of Pan.

They drive their people like a flock of sheep,
Abuse the general, murmur at the odd,
Only cry out, perhaps, at home in sleep,
And may, or they may not, believe in God;
But never had I trouble with one such,
For they were quiet and had traveled much.

From *The City Built on Sand*: No. 10

The clergyman, the rich man, and the teacher,
Each sacred and as dazed as if by drink —
Sin's, poverty's, and ignorance's creature —
Are never told what people really think.
Unto God's vicar businessmen confess
Never their gain, but only how they fail.
The millionaire is sheltered from address,
And pedagogues avoid the county jail.

One time I saw, as Venus doused her lamp,
Some trolleys crawling through a foggy night.
The first was crammed with many a pushing scamp
And folk close-packed; the others traveled light.
So to the chancel, bank, or special class,
Bright empty cars, the unenlightened pass.

From *The City Built on Sand*: No. 16

In another city, far as space can lie
And lie in the same world, yet not so far
That it looks up at any different sky
Or may not watch on one immortal star —
Sirius faithful to Orion's track,
Polaris for an age the seaman's pole —
I left a lady where the brave turn back
And spent a generation with my soul.

Do not believe, dear maiden, I would not
Have haled you thence to Tophet or the Throne:
Far as I wandered, if my flesh forgot,
My recollection kept you for its own;
But much too late and but in dream I see
The destination formed of you and me.

LANDSCAPE

Out of the window flying, the glass mind
Flaps for a moment over the tan marsh,
Straightens its course and heads as if to find
A destination where the copse is harsh
Along the swell of the first bench above
The greenish river, marked by taller sedge.
It flies, a thought, to seek the place of love,
Which sank long since below the daylight's edge.

Were it but large and black of wing and strong,
The mind would soar past trivial slopes and hills
To the blue hollow night already fills
Between the crags of Deadmouth and the long
Jagged upheaval of Sir Mordred's Spine.
These mountains baffle the geologer,
For they were formed expressly to be mine
By the unlawful bubbling of pure fire.

OF NOVEL DISSEIZIN

No place in mountains, either, can be home.
Life-long you might remain there, but in spring
The avalanche comes down, leaving a ring
Of rocks around the ruin, a square hole
With green grass in it summers afterward.

Or build your cabin in a safer spot,
A cave externalized to match the bear's,
And of thick timbers cut in the near wood
With quiet labor: die, and the logs rot
Season by season in the heatless air.

The pig with quills, the rodent of the rocks,
The flower Calypso and the August grass,
Are the true people. Man is the wrong kind,
Belonging elsewhere with the shell and weed.
The fishy ocean weeps to drag him home.

THE WOMAN

Twenty or thirty feet below the summit
Of the peak we were climbing, which has no name on the
      maps,
I acquired misgivings, perfect in their timing,
Such as befall, I suppose, a number of chaps.

No great distance remained, but I became
All of a sudden solicitous and paternal,
And I called my son back from the steps of the last cliff.
He was higher than I, but I looked up and saw the
      infernal,
With black rock splitting a hundred ways to an if.

Far below, a flyspeck in the valley,
I could see the old car I had forced to its last gasp,
Waiting where she was making a fire for us
When we came down without heaven in our grasp.

THE PRANK

Among these mountains dwell the elves of old,
And in their caverns gnomes as well do dwell.
Tales of their shape and line I once was told,
But was made swear that I would never tell.

There went three picnickers to share a lunch
Of wine air-warm and chicken choice and cold.
Within the hills they heard the saplings crunch
And the rocks slide; some little pebbles rolled

Quietly from the gravel bank upright
Behind them where they sat beside a stream.
The two men stared, with each his guilt in sight;
The only woman fetched a soundless scream.

Impending from athwart both north and south
Hung the bent cliffs, improper to misdeem.
The three stood hidden from the canyon-mouth,
And mutually clear as in a dream.

ON BEING TOO BUSY TO ATTEND
ONE'S TWENTY-FIFTH CLASS REUNION

Some in the sun, some in the grimy sea,
Some from natural causes, unlike me,
Would not be back in any case to drink
A toast to days before they learned to think,

While some who have not stirred far from the spot
Will surely be there, while some such will not,
And others, scattered over Terra's face,
May yet return, a few, to view the place

Whence they set out on being well equipped
With higher learning or its parascript.
Unfortunate I, who cannot quite come home
To pseudo-Athens or its captor Rome.

*　　*　　*

Well, in my absence, let me then declare
That which I found in it that appeared fair —
The snow, the grass, the odd and parching mountains,
The vanities and wishes young as fountains,

The beautiful stone, the mud in every alley,
The Nineteenth Century still able to rally —
Whether in chapel or in classroom thoughts
Offered to faces like a row of noughts;

And the undertone — always the undertone —
That the classics were dying. We fought on alone,
I and the professor of both Latin and Greek;
Accepted science, turned the other cheek.

*　　*　　*

You would not guess how many tragic years
I held an image in my heart, of tears
Shed for a marble statue flouted while
Crude engineers contrived a faster mile,

Or bartering merchants, screaming as they sold,
Cheated themselves and bit their leaden gold.
The picture shuddered and I shrank from it,
Nor could have praised it for its truth and wit.

*　　*　　*

But I was wrong, despite my good professor.
Latin not wasted, nor my mind the lesser
For poring on it, I was well advised
To think of Caesar and the works he prized.

Aqueducts bring me water from the hills;
Bridges upbear me while my office fills;
I have Justinian in my head at once
With Coke and Blackstone and the party fronts.

In every client Gaius Gracchus sprouts,
Or his assassin. I have seen the routs
Where Orosius elbows with Thucydides.
Men often ask me questions such as these:

Whose is the body when the head is severed?
Where was Achilles when the tortoise quivered?
Why do the Goths come down all over the place?
When is the future of the human race?

*   *   *

I remember he used to say, "As Horace said . . . "

Now I am rich, though taxed, and he is dead.

AN UNWRITTEN ESSAY OF MONTAIGNE: WHETHER OF THE TWO, METHUSELAH OR TITHONUS LIVED TO BE THE OLDER

If age means full of years, but one lives on
And is no longer young but cannot die —
Is it unkind of him to view the sky
At morning pink, and not to love the dawn?

We have such knowledge from our sources as
Appears to prove the Hebrew lacked a scant
Century of reaching a millennium.   Rant
Makes the Greek immortal, with what a corpse has.

I suppose women are of such stuff as youth
Thinks vital, middle age finds useful, or
Old men can smile on — granddaughter or bore.
Tithonus and Methuselah died happy, that's the truth —

For who would be a senile lover?   I
Suffer the stone; Methuselah circumcised
Is known for nothing but his years. If prized,
Tithonus had them, but he wished to die.

All-kind Jehovah — that is, Zeus — consented
The boon be granted. Well, I call that wisdom.
(You cannot be a god and split the prism,
For the light shines in the colors it is tinted.)

Who cares how old two ancient worthies got?
I do; and yet one day I shall be not.

DIRECTIONS

To reach our house you take a crummy bus
In a small village where white shirts are few.
You ride an hour with Indians or us
Or any else who ride along with you.

Where you alight there is no town or store;
No one will meet you; you can look away
Ten miles at night, a hundred miles by day.
Here no one worries much about a war,

Since by the time an enemy appeared
Across the desert or our alpine east,
Most of the rest of all men would have ceased
To need our succor. For our local fyrd

We have ourselves, our fatalistic friends,
Our visitors from elsewhere, and the hills.
In the spring season every river fills
With the cold water June in Utah sends,

Or bare Wyoming. Come by Jackson Hole;
Fish with the current, cast a skillful fly
Against the wind and in the future's eye,
Feed well and pamper your immortal soul.

We have a house here and a yard and field,
A forest and a patch of mountain peak,
Blankets, a fire, a highway you may seek
To find the quaint or what has lain concealed.

Bring your own meat. We feed ourselves alone
On the sweet berry and the fossil bone.

HAROLD WITT

Born Santa Ana, California, 1923. Attended Santa Ana city schools, Santa Ana Junior College, B.A. from the University of California, Berkeley, 1943; M.A. from the University of Michigan, 1947; B.L.S. (Bachelor of Library Science) from the University of California, Berkeley, 1953. Reference Librarian, Washoe County Library, Reno, Nevada, 1953-55, travel in Europe, 1955, Reference and Documents Librarian, San Jose State College, 1956-59.

Poems and short stories began appearing in literary magazines about 1944, poems published in a wide range of magazines including *Saturday Review, Ladies' Home Journal, The New Yorker, The New Republic, The Nation, The Atlantic, The Kenyon Review, The Carleton Miscellany, Talisman, Poetry, Poetry Northwest, Prairie Schooner, Beloit Poetry Journal, Contact, San Francisco Review, The Massachusetts Review,* etc.

A group of poems appeared in *Eight American Poets,* edited by James Boyer May and published by Villiers, London, 1952. *Family in the Forest,* The Porpoise Bookshop, San Francisco, 1956. *Superman Unbound,* The New Orleans Poetry Journal, 1956. *The Death of Venus,* The Golden Quill Press, Francestown, N.H., Selection of The Book Club for Poetry, 1958. *Beasts in Clothes,* The Macmillan Company, N.Y., 1961.

Hopwood Award for poetry, 1947. Phelan Award for narrative poetry, 1960.

THE DOUBLE BOY

Our hero, Beanstalk Jack, the little lame
prince of sweetness, Oliver of light,
darling David saving from Goliath
good guys by his bullseye, honest George
charmingly chopping cherries years before Valley Forge,

drags a siamese shadow at his back,
a child who's wily, thumbs his gremlin nose
at Dad and Mother, a twin who grinningly lies
and goes in sly disguises, boy of night,
a puckish Huck Finn demon, the dream's dark brat.

Gayer in one way, graver in another,
double entendre Lausbub, than his brother,
his restless presence rather bothers girls —
in the rose of reason the bug of evil lunches;
the delinquent chuckles under Fauntleroy's curls.

A spitting image of the boy who's balancing,
prim as a teacup, politeness on his lap,
behind back fences in his old straw hat
he's tying cans to dogs' tails, torturing cats,
zinging his slingshot through knotholes at pompousness,

whistling in thistles, smoking cigarettes,
sweaty and warted, intimate with worms;
the cool blue woods steam with his casual piss;
he happily strips and, lively, dives through scums,
then lies on his freckled back, naked, in good grass.

HAND ON THE GUN

Hand on the gun the day the cat died—
my father's manly one,
veined and sinewed, touched the trigger,
eternity between

then and the first shot, the first sick kitten
blasted beyond.
Truth in the orchard, death by the mustard
yellow with bees and sun,

virile the jaw at every cocking;
straight from the eye that sighted
bullets tore five furs of pathos—
life could never be righted.

Meowing at last, the pink-tongued mother
whose comfort I had known
twitched to a stillness tears and shaking
wouldn't wake her from.

"The cats were sick. We couldn't keep them,"
he said. "It had to be done,"
and I fell down forever, cold in that clover,
but took his assassin's hand.

FROM AUNTS AND UNCLES

2

Summer and winter my Aunt Lilly sat
chilled in her sunroom reading books of love,
her flesh bright clothed, her bones too deep for heat,
her odd, small body too entranced to move.
Vicarious heroine dancing tall and tense
through ballrooms of intrigue, the nymph of many beds,
she fled across romantic continents
while Uncle Peter multiplied like seeds
her planted cash, the money money breeds;
and she was richer than some princesses
but begged from fiction all her warmer needs
for real desire, for daring instances —
lips at her icy ear, and hands to speed
her heart, not paper, while it still could beat.

3

Now I am uncle, like homunculi
puny nephews, dwarfish nieces sport
comic around me, now instead of me
a later generation just as short
notes my mustachioed eccentricity
as once I stared at Uncle Peter's wart,
as, from the vantage of a lower eye,
normal faces frequently distort.
I view them not as children, but as some
funny show of quick and charming freaks,
knowing my own enlargement looks to them
one of those natural, disturbing quirks
—humorous animal, or man from space—
and neither dreams the other in his place.

SOME LIVES

Some lives have ruined layers, Troys below
slow mound barren meetings of the eye
lie dump heap palaces, onetime walls —
Cassandra chanted wildhaired prophecy,
breastplate heroes clattered in the halls
vivid burnings melted like a snow.
Some lives are fossiled with a buried glow.

Some lives rise more Egyptian, slipped in sand
great shapes still visible though chipped conceal
tombs of faience, sarcophagi of gold,
jewel masked Pharaohs who in marvelous murals
are punted huntward, recognizable.
You see the very bone beneath the hand
that held regality; the lilied Nile

flows continuous, as green as real.
And there are lives like wrecked, conjectured Rome,
broken forum steps that lead you up
to nothing but a single perfect column,
alleys of headless vestals, a stone lap
that has no breast or face; you only feel
a certain glory vanished from the rubble.

And then in this sad chronicle at last,
this list of lives, come some of pinnacles,
structures windowed gold and dipped in dawn,
with swirls of glass and color being built,
harplike bridges to a rivered island
sapphire at night, not yet a ghost
of shattered splendor in a present past.

AT TIMES, FOUR FOOTED

At times, four footed in my barking garden,
best friends battle, thoroughbred and cur
lick, whine, snarl, growl, and snap in fur —
unembarrassed, they are often ardent;
frequently lifting legs, they snuffle and sniff,
loll drooling tongues at young frustration's bitch,

the virgin beagle rolling under their noses
her scent of not yet readiness, her teats
buttoning up her belly's future heats.
Aromas rich to us as seas and roses
waft high adventure on the animal winds;
vying to be top dog, they tear and twist.

Yet whistled home, they pad obediently back,
teeth sheathed, with friendly whisker, claw in paw,
sit up, woof meekly, wolfish if at all
only at danger's dinner, won't attack;
mild and silken, ferocity that wags
a tail of tameness singled from the pack.

IN SENSUOUS SOUTHS

In sensuous souths, a Mexico of youth,
a beach boy burned and burnished, slow at pearl,
I dove blue deeps for nothing but the truth,
dripped back to pebbled edges where a girl
laughed at my patient emptyhandedness.
She guessed I'd give it up and went along,
unconvinced that my lithe sandiness
presaged a lifetime of such goings on.
She waited humming while I bubbled down,
thinking she'd last my failure into doubt
then change me over into anyman,
but wasn't there when I came shouting out
lugging a shellshape shoreward, which revealed,
egg big at last, maturity concealed.

FROM RUSHMORE AND EASTWARD

1. RUSHMORE

Rushing to Rushmore, speeding as we read
sphinx comparisons (in the free brochure)
to monumental features of the dead,
we doubted art in such a spacious sculpture

especially done by dynamite and drill,
smirked that workmen with electric hammers
had hacked a factual grandeur from that hill.
We sneered like critics. What did those amateurs,

exploding crude colossi out of stone,
know of Cellini and his detailed golds,
David expressive to the very tendon
or marble Grecians rippling in their robes?

And we were anxious on a trip to elsewhere,
winding narrowness, just to glimpse and go.
Then through a tunnel we saw history centered,
staring four faced, bluish in the glow.

Dazzled travelers, skeptic to the end,
we drove up closer, looked in Lincoln's eye
in which a six foot man could easily stand
and, vita brevis, made a longer stay.

We gazed along the precipice of faces,
silenced by a pyramidal shock—
temples, obelisks, the statued ages
were equaled in that democratic rock.

3. DUBUQUE

When I went through Dubuque only in August
nothing of summer thinned the solid town;
hips of housewives before their ugly houses
stuck in the frozen heat, belly and frown

bulged, gouged; I thought of Sinclair Lewis
protesting middlewestness: there it was —
brick-bleak and blank, the fragile druggist
preserved in ancient ennui under glass.

Nothing of leaves or lightness, though there were
      leaves,
saved from dull geometries of gloom
bare flat houses on their squares like lives
identically windowed, and little light let in.

There were no flowers flaring for that funeral;
the grievers in a loss of afternoon
hardly knew they mourned; the good, the beautiful
rotted, in strict extinction, underground.

4. INSIDE IOWA

Thundering Iowa hissed a hostile rain
as if at us, the dark dragon of weather
forking tongues of lightning over corn,
and we slowed down, sliding through the splatter,

feeling our wheels go slick as rolling pigs.
We blinked for signs of coffee, lit cafes
to warm us from a leaking harm like dikes
but towns and farms slipped deeper in that haze.

The cornbins glistened and the silos flashed
pictures in a tungsten suddenness;
the tails of the stormy monster lashed
flickering scales across the muddiness.

Then at a deluged corner, warehouse-square,
a coalsmoke restaurant, brick and hardly lettered,
next to a factory for fertilizer
spelled oasis, stark, old, dark and battered.

We ran around the building in the rain
like figures in a nightmare, trying doors,
and all were locked except the magic one
that opened on a sesame of mirrors,

pink lights, rich carpets, politesse,
a maitre d'hotel bowing from the gilt —
laconic Iowa or ironic Paris?
We rested among graciousness, and felt

a friendliness replenishing our cups,
the difference of interiors, a dream
of shelter from the mire of the maps
that only showed us where we hadn't been.

THE NOBLE SAVAGE

I met an Indian in a latrine—
that flush reminded of high waterfalls,
Hiawatha by a spotted fawn—
fat, watery eyes tattooed with red.
He wore a cowboy hat and jeans,
reeking of cheapest wine.

I thought papooses and beaded
braids and pots and dyed designs,
a chief in feathers, leather legs
of braves in leather moccasins—
and then, museums of the dead,
a Salt Lake bowl with mummy grain.

He asked me only, "Got a dime?"
stumbling by the scrawled-on wall
in stolen boots, Ramona's man
fattened, had he lived, by time.
And gave the money as they gave
trinkets for an island once.

ECHO, ECHO

Skipping the lake a glacier scooped from granite,
the speedboat slows, turning through reflection—
a channel out of Echo into Echo,
lake linked to lake but not a repetition.
Smaller in stone, the second lake laps quiet
at rocky islands as a thought can change
blatant blues to lilac subtleties,
a wild water stilled and tinted strange.

We disembark and wave the boat away
that spreads a water peacock in its wake,
and walk and look, alone on a tiny island.
Our doppelgängers picnic in the lake
and clouds scud twice, once above the mountains,
again across the ghost sun in the lake
that breaks to such a spectral flow of patterns
the granite world is lake-changed where we look—

nothing the same, as in a dream's dimension,
the hush we wished, the peace we only hoped
echo the landscapes of the waking day.
It is ourselves, and not the earth that stopped
speeding through space, and quiet on an island,
cloud, tree, water, stone in each direction,
we find in mirrored mountains of the mind
reason enough for time, enough time for reflection.

WORLD'S END AT POINT RICHMOND

Hundreds of gulls that never heard prediction
rise from feeding on roe, whir both ways at once,
some in one, some in another direction,
settling again, like the pause in an endless dance
or winter snows before spring's resurrection.

There is a world end weirdness to the light,
the glitter about to eclipse, the ripples of rose
glimmering shoreward as if toward final night,
as anything beautiful seems about to disclose
absolute answers to relative questions of sight.

We raise red wine in glasses of tulip shape
against the misted bay still rimming bright
(while Hindus panic and others have lost all hope)
feel sure our children canoeing in silhouette
will reach the beach, however brittle the boat.

Churchbells faintly float, whistles and foghorns blow
in the lessening glow like notes by Bela Bartok—
once more the gulls flap up from their feasts of roe
timed to an accurate need beyond the clock,
and shadow sliced, the sun is beginning to go.

Planets like patience took twenty thousands years
looping ellipses summoned by the sun
to make this line that superstition fears,
and now our goggled children are taking it in,
a circle of dark where brightness disappears,

but not completely; the water continues to shimmer,
the gulls could not care less what science knows;
it was only an interlude, too, that differed our dinner
and another mistake so easily made by those
believing in ends when ends are only a pause.

OTHER WORDS FOR A
UNITED NATIONS CHRISTMAS CARD

The frosted golf course gleams beside the highway,
corpses of run-down deer stare stiff where the fog thins—
as if they could, robins fly a sparkling
sapphire dome of frozen seeming sky.
What fearless message can I send this year
when bombs grow bigger, and a neighbor's shovel
digs ignorant shelter from the dangerous air?

He'll strike it rich or reach a childhood China
before he's safe from fallouts of his fear.
The trees were iced this almost Christmas morning,
the final leaves were dropping into winter—
a bad day for digging, but my neighbor
thought hot armpits and a sweating foot,
the jigging exercise of his manual labor,

like beating a gong at the time of an eclipse
to make the dark disk slip across the sun,
would keep off cataclysm, or at least could scoop
a grave for life beneath the poison mushroom.
He needs more than a fat pastel fish
(children's faces for scales) playing a violin
to smile him from this rut that he is in.

A friendly greeting in several languages,
carefully worded and not offending anyone,
won't send insight down his black abyss.
He's sure that every terror's deep as his.
Efforts at peace especially look suspicious;
there's nowhere else to go but underground—
unless it's lightward, not like starstruck Magi

but toward a different Christmas closer home,
forgetting tinsel and the swaddled infant—
music, nature, friendship, all will do
to set the longrun good against the instant
imagined evil when a bomb might blow
good neighbor, bad neighbor equally helterskelter,
and scatter us shelterless in an active glow.

Still, I think he prefers the usual light.
He might even see, as I do, if he looked up,
peachsticks changed to whiteness overnight,
the web of frost that's spun from tip to tip
beginning to drip wet jewelry on the fence—
it could just make the difference, if he did,
between wanting to crouch in his cave or stay outside.

KILLER

Beneath black headlines here is a face of dots,
the average looking killer grim in glasses.
This undistinguished hand that fired the shots
triggers our thoughts: all faces smile suspicious.

The story mentions failure; many fail.
The murderer confesses God told him to do it.
Now he is safely martyred. Bums in jail
hammer him up with words that persecute.

Didn't he have a Bible in his pocket?
Hadn't he left behind the classic clue?
Wasn't most of his glory in being caught?
He says he's sorry. Is there anything new?

I AM ENJOYING POETRY AGAIN

I am enjoying poetry again.
For a while it seemed words, words; I mean,
its overwhelming question, the news from academe,
far from the madding crowd in which I lived
of desperation's suburb, then long rains daffodilled

the brickwalks, flamed me with something camellia —
a scent like Brahms blew from the festering mulch;
I thought I was over that, but it horned my evening,
its beating tympani metered like a heart —
and just the other day, shoveling the leaf rot,

as I turned that fetid darkness into the sun,
a deathwhite spider danced away from the worms
and I thought, or felt rather than thought—
that's it — poetry's belowness,
the sowbug underside, whether it rhymes or not,

form can't ignore or any love leave out,
the deaths we walk on like layers of leaves
endless centuries shed from a central tree
but the tree greening, spreading oaken as ever
Euripides, Shakespeare, everywhere I read.

POETS I KNOW

suffer as much as Shelley—
handsome as a villain, one jumped from a bridge.
Most like liquor, women, walks in woods.
No one loves them enough except themselves.

If they are women, they aren't exactly wives—
traumatic Emilys married to the sun,
they're partly flesh and mostly butterflies.
They cry like rain, to glisten everyone

and burst perfumes along the freshened branch.
Experience is where they went for stanzas.
They don't live here but in a town of time.
Reims will bong a singsong for their rhyme

or not-rhyme; some would rather die
than starve the hungry ear with June and moon.
Often they're learned, doctors of the odd;
can tell you what it is, but can't tell why.

Dantes, they will Virgil you through hell
and then contrast a too-bright paradise,
Shakespeares, bees, they break with able eyes
every landscape to the shapes that thrill.

Visit at risk their green, deceiving gardens,
scan with care the image that they show—
both fly of truth that's destined to be dinner
and cocked and hazardous lizard might be you.

DREAMSCAPE IN KÜMMEL

Upward through crystal in a kümmel bottle
a bare sprig branched into the vacancy
and I was climbing, fly-size, in that subtle
odd liqueur, up a flavor tree
on limbs so brittle that I thought I'd fall.

I held on helpless, lost, like dwindled Alice,
calling through thick sweet emptiness for aid
while all the bulging faces through the glass
dream or womb I hung in smiled and made
wavering pantomimes of friendliness.

And it was easy for the ones outside
to toast my plight with their complacent *crème;*
they only tasted from the other side,
sipping tiny samples on a stem,
the loneliness that I was drowning in.

ALAN STEPHENS

For the first eighteen years of my life I lived on a small farm near the town of Greeley in northern Colorado. During the winters I went to school in the town, during the summers I worked on the farm. In 1943, when I was eighteen, I went into the U.S. Army Air Force, and after the war I entered the University of Colorado. I have been associated with one university or another ever since; at present I am teaching at the University of California at Santa Barbara. I am married, and my wife and I have three sons.

I write verse slowly and haltingly, and, as I imagine it, under the impartial supervision of those rules of discourse which I have come to respect. In general I aim for lucidity and force, for a style that will go about disclosing its materials without itself becoming conspicuous, for a tone that seems neither too exalted nor too casual to belong in the central regions of my experience. Though I customarily have several friends in mind as I write, I have them in mind because I admire their grasp of the rules. When those rules fall into satisfied silence over cadences, syntax, and the rest, I can feel that the poem is completed. Usually the silence that follows a final bout of composition is more or less morose.

103

A BRIEF INVOCATION

Be with me, powers
  of the tongue I love,

sources of clarity in
  the turns of life:

that the slow action of the
  understanding and the motions

of the rapid feelings
  breathe in a unison—
health howsoever brief.

THE MORNING PEACE

The two cats drowse. Still warm, the silverware
Is in the chest, the swept floor glows, the noise
Of wife and small sons leaving for the park
Recedes, and each room stands in steadied air.
But quick—his thought, just coming into poise,
Is due in verse, quiet as a remark
That he might make now if his wife were there,
And the clear square of light where the cats drowse
Moves on, the corner cools in the half dark.

A WALK IN THE VOID

I could not see the life I live.
Wheeling to catch it as it was,
I found myself the fugitive;
There were my footprints, in reverse.
I could not praise them, could not curse.
Bare of their principle and cause,

They lay caught fast within that realm
No inquiry can justify,
No good or evil overwhelm.
To enter was to be interred
Where the gross lip absorbs the word.
It was what dead men occupy.

Or so it seemed. And yet I live.
Living I left my tracings there.
Driven historian, I arrive
Here where I blindly went, and see.
Dark walker through dubiety!—
Resuming you I grow aware,

Which is my life. O formless ground
Of quick experience, but not
Experience itself, I found
That I had walked upon thy void
Saved by the blindness I employed
Till I stood blinking in my thought.

THE SUM

What do the living keep?
Once I had learned to hide
In my own place, and shape
Distinctions out of it,
The indiscriminate
Washed in from every side,

And lo, I had endured
Beyond what I had done.
The purport was secured
But not the man. The man,
Where the purport began,
Is an indifferent one—

Having no proper name,
His function is to die;
All potency, no form,
And not respectable;
Still, he is tough. And while
We live, my one ally.

—Friend, now that I must go
Think back on how I came
A bare appearance. Now,
Am I not such again,
In leaving? In between
Came work, and talk, in time.

Since the mere time is past
And yet was friendship's ground,
Take what I've written best
As what I'd leave you with,
As but a kind of death
Elsewhere than in your mind.

This kept, discount the man
That enters on the chill
Other, where he began.
Should weakness make him strange,
Or chance, or a better change,
We've known of such; farewell.

WRITTEN FROM A GROVE

Here all's enclosed; for seven days
I've camped in this blue-shaded wood—
My study and my scholar ways
Vacated; I have played the mute,
Lone with perception as the brute,
Whose world is in him, understood.

And all's defined and done: I note
The blue-glazed wing, the striped fur,
The incised hoof and creamy throat—
If the beginning was a word
These are the end, who never heard.
Moment on moment, they occur.

Should but one concept, alien, knock
At the creation they contain,
They are so hearted that the shock
Would bring not death, their common care,
But sudden indifference in the air,
And the creation to explain.

Quick to their sweet necessity
(As I work backward into speech)
The wild bees bend the timothy,
Take, and depart. I name and know,
Take in the distance where they go,
Bring bright creation within reach.

"YOU NEED A CHANGE OF SCENE"

Sick of the slippery rot old oaks beget,
The spongy browns of a summer sunken, wet
Leafy destructions, all the heavy smell,
The heavy going of the trees to hell,
I thought of the desert—sand, merely, and air,
The white region of sun, brilliant, bare,
In all directions blank simplicity . . .
Good lack I sought, have I come close? I see
The wiry greasewood; scrub; pale trees whose trunks
Choke off in mistletoe; the riddled chunks
Of cactus snapped, or leaning, hovering rife
With angry dying trapped in angrier life—
But nearer, now, the sun burns sure and bare,
Sure because bare. Let his stare be my stare.

URBAN MORAL

My eyes, barbarian, innocent,
Are helpless. Towers and flanking trees
Rise as a simple incident
With which bright smoke in sun suspended,
Sleek boulevards, thick factories,
The crowd, my coat, my hands are blent—
One plane of shades and lucencies.

Trapped by a surface like the child
That lifts a portrait from the wall
And looks behind it with a wild
Wish that the spirit be extended,
I spin with terror's harsh recoil,
Curse, and assert myself exiled—
City, forgive this animal.

For when at other times I've run
To the impartial, simple ground
And watched it work—beneath the sun
Inwardly self-destroyed, self-mended—
And listened well, what have I found?
Not this nor that; till having grown
Quiet and quieter, I returned,

Relearned the near detail, the play
Of stone and steel, of silk and leather
Bulging with motive. I shall stay,
Knowing the noise begun and ended
In stubborn shapes that calmly weather.
Tentative, ignorant, the way
The soul and body hold together.

VARIATION ON A THEME BY BAUDELAIRE

Now I will write of you; later, with luck,
During calm evenings in another age
My craft will loosen readers of this page
To revery. Adrift like quiet smoke
In each room, you who would leap back and blur
At the breath of scholarly exactitudes
Will tire them, moving willingly with their moods,
Though fastened amongst my rhythms as you were:

Sweet brown-eyed woman, neither wife nor whore
To anybody — you whom I alone
On those calm evenings could still answer for —
Nimble and grave with love there at each door,
Uttering only love — your monotone
Leaving each reader sitting as before.

HOMILY

The desert runs dead-level to the place.
Abstracted, in a smooth reptilian gleam,
The asphalt highway readily climbs and coils
Into a blank commotion of tan stone.

There is a broken sameness everywhere.
Severance, collapse and slippage, rupture, shock
Have long ceased, stone-involved. Through permanence
Of stone held down and locked in other stone,

Brief traveler, regard those ancients, praise
The mind that quickly enters, quickly leaves.

THE DAIMON'S ADVICE

So you of the slow-changing room
That each day you had wakened in
To be your own, provisional,
Slyly-known fellow, tried the sill,
Slipped out, renounced what you had been,
To tamper with this sourceless calm.

How long ago? you ask. But time,
The even circling round a center,
Has nothing here to circle through.
Where movement's neither false nor true,
To turn is not to leave, or enter,
But to stand, tenser yet, the same.

No, you must practice unconcern.
It will not do to glare, and call
Thunder to break from lightning-crack
That the world, at once, come densely back—
You'll owe to some stray, prose detail
Your unremarkable return.

DON JUAN IN HELL
(from the French of Baudelaire)

When Juan reached the netherworld's dark beach
And paid his coin to Charon—a proud Moor,
A beggar with a strong vindictive reach,
Bent forward quickly and took up each oar.

Their blouses open, drooping breasts displayed,
Women beneath the low black firmament
Huddled like sacrifices to be made.
After him their protracted moaning blent.

Sganarelle came smiling for his pay.
Don Luis aimed a trembling finger there
To show the dead that straggled along the way
The impudent son who mocked his whitened hair.

Shaken with grief, Elvira, meager, chaste,
Approached her one-time love, betrayer now,
As if to supplicate him from a last
Sense of the sweetness in his former vow.

A great stone man in armor rose aboard
And took the helm and cut the flowing black.
But the calm hero rested on his sword,
Noticing none of these, and watched the wake.

ANNIVERSARY SEQUENCE

Nil . . . natumst in corpore, ut uti
Possemus, sed quod natumst id procreat usum.

1

If you find bitterness
In this, which ten years late
I place in speech, the source
Is that some trivial force,
Now spent, connected us
Who were so badly taught.

Enough. Searching alone
I could not find the cause
Of the first touch. I turned,
Wrote what I since had learned—
You like a minor clause
Had fixed the final tone.

2

No matter, which we chose;
Eros or mystic Rose
Conjured us to discover
The knower from the lover,
Then, with much holy bother,
Lost us in one another.

I thought, the old Chinese
Have subtilized love best:
It is the body's need.
Let love, high kin of thirst
And sleepiness, be led
Gently toward learned ease.

3

But could we lead it so?
—Quick animal, it scared
When the strange mind appeared.
Nor could it learn. Yet, slow,
Our fingers could close round,
Check its erratic bound,

And then, in time, restore
Its trust. Look: wary still
As marriage brings slow years
And as the slow mind clears,
The heart is quiet, small,
As if we were not there.

4

So, when the house is still,
Love works without alarm
Toward his own ends, though we
Give him a time to be;
And though we keep him warm
He is impersonal.

This child, who is an end
Of love, is so contained;
See: his unrippled sleep,
And his loud waking, keep
To their own way. Our care
But guards the going there.

5

We learned all this together.
Now we may let it be.
Now we may move apart
At ease with one another
Into the change of day,
And, changed, come back by heart.

You from the brief detail,
The close quotidian
And ground of sustenance;
I from my thoughts, that tell
In bare significance
What is already gone.

6

—But to curse time, to chafe
At the down-spinning leaf,
Argues that we should rage
At every shift of air,
And back, each day, toward age
Astonished by despair.

Simplicity is best.
Ancient materialist,
The heart occurs, and dies,
Dark, under reason's eyes.
And reason loves the true.
Let us so see love through.

VISITOR

This morning air, shining and equable
Under the tawny beams, along the wall
    Where I have put the books I need,
Wins me once more to the stilled actual.
I lean in pleasure. The season forms outside—
    Dry soil and hardening seed.

An old friend, unannounced. I let him in.
He looks politely at where I have been
    These years, looks at my sons and wife.
I know him by his altered face again,
He knows me by the altering in my life,
    We part with some relief.

In the new calm of the cleared place I knew
I find that commonplace visit coming true
   In rustlings I did not invite.
They shift me; pride or no pride, friend, I too
Have been these years inhabiting my fate,
   Keeping myself in sight.

PROLOGUE: MOMENTS IN A GLADE

Abiding snake:
         At thirty four,
By unset spirit driven here
I watch the season. Warily
My private senses start to alter,
Emerging, at no sign from me,
In the stone colors of my matter.

You that I met in a dim path,
Exact responder with a wrath
Wise in conditions, long secure,
Settled expertly for the kill
You keep a dull exterior
Over quick fiber holding still . . .

Rocking a little, in a coarse
Glitter beneath fine, vacant space,
The hillside scrub oak interlocked
Where year by year, and unattended,
And by abrasive forcings raked
Against itself, it had ascended.

And yet below me sixty feet
A well of air stood dark and sweet
Over clean boulders and a spring.
And I descended through a ripple
Of upper leaves, till noticing
That a rock-pattern had grown supple,

And whirred, I quietly backed off.
I have considered you enough.
The rattle stopped; the rigid coil,
Rustling, began to flow; the head,
Still watching me, swayed down to crawl,
Tilting dead leaves on either side.

You in the adventitious there,
Passion; but passion making sure,
Attending singly what it chose
And so condemned to lie in wait
Stilled in variety — to doze
Or wake as seasons fluctuate,

Eyes open always, the warm prey
At best but happening your way.
And I too slowly found a stone
To break your spine; and I have known
That what I will have surely spoken
Abides thus — may be yet thus broken.

A PASTORAL
taken from John Muir's Sierra diary

1
Toward the central peaks

Muir spent this summer ninety years ago
(But in a city, later, lived and died):
Singular and unsimplified and slow
The sheep come down along the dry hillside,
Making the sagebrush lightly quiver; low
And mild the colors and the sounds subside,
Venus descending in gray-amethyst;
The dogs lying down; the near hills darkening fast.

Now for the quiet of the minimal.
Far up the valley — like a nearing thought
The dark air comes down on the black detail —
To be by practised waking movement brought
Against the severe peace of the mineral,
The early June night glittering in the drought
That brings the soil hot yellow under dawn,
Sheep coughing in the dust they forage on.

And by midmorning crows drop to the ground
For solid oak-shade, and the cottontail
Retreat from shade to shade: the flock has wound
Past wavering foothills sprung from broken shale
Through the first pines and spruces. And beyond,
The sharp feet inching up as grasses fail,
Where clouds are white and firm, and the streams cold,
Ferns lean with icy lilies in black mould.

2
Visitors, denizens

Brief grazing here, for sheep; and noiselessly
The long days close and open, shining air

Is prime, and now the old simplicity,
The anciently attended, quiet there,
Nibbles and spreads — a feeling, edging free
(Panic or peace — and helpless, and entire)
Into the instant, which the brambles block;
A stale bear scent hangs over warming rock.

The scent draws freshly through a stand of fir.
The dog trembles and stops. The bear stands still,
Erect; the larkspurs touch his belly hair.
He lives here, and he walks on up the hill.
Another smelled the flock and shuffled near;
The herder fired, the bear rose up to feel,
With arms thrown out, some body in the hush,
And pondered, and turned back into the brush.

And Paiutes live below, along the streams
That smoothly enter dead salt Mono Lake.
They come for loads of acorns. Granite gleams
Where they ascend, the arctic daisies shake;
They draw near silently; between the seams
Of each wide face the soil is old and thick.
Half-happy, blurred in rabbit-skins, to lie
Beneath ripe bushes; steady, the dark eye.

3
Delays and returns

Late August frost kills out the smaller flies,
The squirrels work rapidly in the conifers,
The creeks grow quiet, and the late grass dries.
A blizzard could break now on lingerers.
The fattened flock works down — the forest lies
Above them, and beyond the lower spurs,
Beyond the last brown thickets, they regain
(Spreading in slow combustion) the bright plain.

Later an earthen swell folds over them.
And consciousness, the lingerer, endures
Back in the heights a savage tedium:
Through morning air adrift with ripened spores
A squall, and trunks left dark in water film
Stand quiet on an open peak that bares
The stone roots caught beneath its streaming flank,
Matter in clean possession of the blank,

With the immoderate light that falls here first:
Here the whole pine grove, which a slow wind slants,
Brings with a stiff and downward flash a burst
Of white against the lance and counterlance
In the hard fragments where the light's reversed.
Down feldspar, quartz and mica, trickles glance,
Sliding to basins pressed in polished stone.
Pastoral extreme — this glistening rough cone.

* * *

So, Muir, that crystalline passivity
Remains; and old simplicity may flow
Up to it still, withdraw, and no more be;
Though as it clears into my words, I know
It's no beginning and no end for me,
Yet sends an undersilence where I go,
Which is like peace in work as I am fit,
My death, like yours, to come far off from it.

ENCOUNTERS

Grandiras-tu toujours, grand arbre plus vivace
Que le cypres?

— Baudelaire, "Le Voyage"

I

On coming to mid-life, I met at last
The Prince of the Air. How patiently obscure,
He said, he'd dogged each stilled particular
Of action where I'd made my nature fast.
   He stopped me in broad day
With intimations: a road that bent away
Into a point stretched back from which I'll cease;
Then, as alternative, he had me see
In steep blue air, above clear shade, a tree —
Lavish and thrusting multiplicity
   Stayed by the deep trunk's ease.

II

I am done with visions, Prince. Alive between
Bare principle, which is not anywhere,
And a continual mineral grip as bare,
I use for what I see the grades of green
   In my oak, fir, and bay.
They fill the yard; I watch them slowly sway.
The early undifferentiated light,
The evening fog that comes in off the sea,
Touching my trees' clear veined variety
Break down, and blur in slow emergency
   Motioning day and night.

III

The good of time on earth is what I sought.
Virtue and meaning should accumulate.
You say the lone action is a death, to wait
Is yet another death, and I am caught.

The earth has long been yours,
Familiar Prince. A man learns he secures
His life by leaving it, and then he goes
Alertly in his keen indifference.
I knelt this afternoon beside my fence,
A dozen steady violets cleared my sense,
   After a time I rose.

IV

Blue-lavender above the wet peat moss
They stand out there tonight; three inches tall,
They glisten in the squares of light that fall
Against them from the window through the space
   Between us now; the scent,
Faint and exact, stands out a foot, unspent.
I walked away from it through the plain air.
—Friends at my gate, and men on business,
Find intimations stirring less and less
Through the asperity of the happiness
   In which I greet them there.

GEORGE ELLIOTT

I was born on June 16, 1918, in Knightstown, Indiana. In 1928 my parents moved to a Carob Plantation in the desert near Riverside, California. There, having very little else to do, no money and no neighbors, I read much and took it into my head to write. I began writing stories and poems at the age of fifteen and have never stopped. My father was a farmer. I am the oldest of four children.

I graduated from the Riverside Junior College in 1937 and came to the University of California in Berkeley. I got my M.A. in English in 1941. In that year, I married Mary Emma Jeffress, and in 1943 our only child, Nora, was born.

During the war, I worked in the Richmond Shipyards, in the War Labor Board, and for the Technical Engineers, Architects, and Draftsmen Union (AFL). After the war I worked as a surveyor's helper, a labor paper reporter, a real estate broker, and a taxi driver. In 1947 I began teaching at St. Mary's College, where I stayed until 1955. I taught at Cornell University 1955-56, at Barnard College 1957-60, at the Writers Workshop of the State University of Iowa 1960-61, and at the University of California in Berkeley in the spring of 1962; in the fall I returned to St. Mary's College, and in 1963 went to Syracuse University.

I have been awarded a Bender Literary Grant-in-Aid, a Fellowship by the Fund for the Advancement of Education, a Hudson Review Fellowship in Fiction, and a Guggenheim Fellowship.

122

I edited *Fifteen Modern American Poets* (Rinehart Editions, 1956). I have published some forty stories, nearly all in literary magazines; ten of them are collected in *Among the Dangs* (Holt, Rinehart and Winston, 1961). I have published over sixty poems in magazines, and a long narrative poem in book form, *Fever and Chills* (Stone Wall Press, 1961). I have also published a number of book reviews, informal essays, and literary essays, and two novels, *Parktilden Village* (Beacon, 1958) and *David Knudsen* (Random House, 1962).

FIVE-IN-ONE

Through a curtain blurring the windowpane I saw
Dancers with round combs in their hair,
The five of them with a single-echoing step
Leaving the town's useful streets.

I doubted as they hurried that the proper road
Was graded thus, level and ruled,
Or that its fence would zigzag like law so sharply.
They tugged a long shadow after.

I turned them toward the crumbling ledges of a bluff
Down which they stumbled their own path,
Lightened by the laughter of a glistening girl
Running away up the veined surf.

I argued that the sea-path of the moon's beauty
Moving unchanged, so, as they moved
Was the bone of her dance and the way of their way;
They came to the wet shore with me.

As we paused for miles by the silencing breakers
Moon's mounting shortened their shadow,
A radiance unusable on the smooth sand
Haloing five-in-one our head.

TO A BIRD OUTSIDE THE WINDOW

Little bird, I do not know
What you are called or why you sing;
I do not know, when winter comes,
What you will fear or where you'll go.

I rarely touch the world you're in;
Ill at ease I hear you now.
You like money call to mind
A life which I have only seen.

WHEN WARM AND
STRANGEING MOONLIGHT

When warm and strangeing moonlight
Has bared your back of clothing,
A marvel in your motions
    As pin by pin
    Your hair falls down
Impels to your raised arms my sculpturing hands.

Last night when sleep dissuaded
Your body from its flaunting,
Such order curved your fingers,
    Such peace disposed
    Your arching throat,
As stilled for bending hours my gandering heart.

Why do you toss your head so
That for a whirling moment
Your hair becomes a halo?
    Why turn sometimes,
    Inward from me,
Behind a veil of curls, your brilliant eyes?

I, whom your touch has toppled
Headlong into deep yearning,
Would safeguard from time's scatter,
    Long as may be,
    That which in you
Fills, to my drowning joy, your perishing flesh.

That which in you mosaics
Plain atoms in bright gestures
Can so set words in verses,
    If so it will,
    That one who reads
May find here, fixed and silent, flashings of you.

The self of your exulting
Demands my kneeling praises;
And I have knelt to please it;
    But this has raised
    Me mute with joy —
A selfless turn of your victorious wrist.

A DAY OFF

Profiles of mountains slice the clean sky.
At the window when I take a deep breath
Bubbles no bigger than pinheads explode
Up and bright in my nose. The children jump;
They bruise their shouts against four-story walls;
They lob dry clods from behind the garage
Onto the concrete driveway crumblingly.

Dear, wash some celery, butter some bread,
Broil a couple of chickens, and put in the salt;
And I'll go get some olives and sharp cheese,
Wine, paper napkins, pop for the kids, grapes,
And pack a camp-chair in the car for Jo
If she'll come; and we'll spring-trespass again
On the Water District's fenced, pleasant fields.

Phyllis's voice, keen and up in her head,
Traces its melodies with a fine edge;
Barney, when he plays his sweet recorder,
Whets back and forth, his shirt off, his brown hair
Tangled as a goat's, prancing as he flutes.
We'll phone them; they'll want to go to the beach,
Find tidepools, loll around a driftwood fire —

But sky for the day is lightened of lead,
Sun's hot: we'll drive them out the Bear Creek Road
And jounce through gullies in a farmer's ruts
To a cluster of unpruned cherry trees,
A green picnic by an abandoned shed.
We'll gulp the bubbling air, we'll watch the kids
Leap through the meadow grass chasing the cows,

Jo will mount butterflies on her sharp words,
Phyllis will wend through tunes, Barney will skip,
We'll all get high. Maybe this afternoon,
As on the day we first happened upon
That mottling shade at the foot of a hill,
Petals of blossoms shaken by a gust
Will scatter over us, light in your hair.

SPELUNKER

He bruises his way through holes,
Climbs cliffs, and swims black rivers:
To find, to his pure joy,
A room of flints and bones,
Brute ancestors, brute others.
Were they not others surely
Who threw their spears at pictured
Buffalo on the walls
Or chopped their fingers off
To ease famine, darkness,
The long advance of ice?

BLIND

So long as memory of the seen world
Bruised me, crushed blossoms in my fist,
Kicked the curb that tripped me, they watched me;
But after my rage turned into a cane
Swishing, they gave me a dog to see with.

Blind is not dark. I am a hand —
I squeeze oranges, learn the hands I shake,
With two fingers I can open and stitch up a heart —
Yet a hand shown by the harness of a dog.
My dog stinks, he strains after bitches.

They told me, Teach your blind hand
The feel of a dog if you want to see;
Scratch him behind the ears and he'll step you up curbs;
Roll with him on the lawn, tousle him, butt him.
He jumps up licking, and I've got to like it.

A hand is all there: I am part of a man.
Even when my head bumps on a branch
That he's neglected to duck for me, I've got to roughhouse
     him,
To stroke him though his hairs are harsh to my hand.
No other way: I must love to see.

Yet, last week when he was sick, I missed
Him, not his seeing for me but hugging him,
Brushing him, slapping his sides, trusting him.
He is the rest of me. He whines when I nuzzle him.
He's taught me to love by hand as I go.

HIS CATARACT IS REMOVED, LETTING THE LIGHT IN

Since it is up, and dizzingly bright,
That is the sky; and that, because spray in the air
And sounds of scrape and smash come from it,
That band of broken, unresting greens is the sea.

On the sand, at a damp mound, I notice twins,
Oblongs of beach-life, reversed identicals,
Glowing, (as everything glows); I touch to learn:
Feet: whose head shouts "What's the matter with you?"

It's long as my forearm, pointed, and pale green.
With my eyes shut I smell it: eucalyptus;
Lift it: a leaf.   But light is all if you look—
This grey sand flea, this twig's brown socket: light, light.

Love's touchings have taught me the texture of your
        roundness;
But which of these in white and blue bathing suits,
Dazzling beyond identity, can you be?
How could my blindness have learned your shades of
        brown?

His red and blue umbrella tilts cornerless;
His robe is yellow, his hair black smoothing to grey,
And the dusted black of his skin is netted with cracks;
Only if I touch him could I guess his age;

Meanwhile I love him because he radiates
Glory — not his, yet without him not.
Glory is what I hope never to learn,
The making light visible on, say, you.

PHOTOGRAPHER TO LADY

Long experience with nudes
Stretched in famous attitudes,
Mounded for a lover's kiss,
Swooned on rugs, has taught me this:
Would-be wanton, you should pose
In the privacy of clothes.
Stony-naked promises
Crush the buds of wantonness,
But a suitable attire
Can unfurl the full desire.
You are pure in public skin
As a nun robed in from sin.

You, who show your nudity
At expense of modesty,
Must assume, or think you must,
Postures of marmorean lust.
Limbs should move in molds of will
Temporal and violable —
Public looking locks the thighs.
Nearness closes lovers' eyes,
But the public lips of kiss
Part in geometric bliss.
Darkling, lady, your bright breast
Stirs the hungering hand to rest.

READING SOME MATERIALISTS

The matter which embodies me
Is not my anchor mired in sin
But what must surely set me free,
If I am brave as those have been.

Well, I am free enough to guess
What gears grind out my happiness,
And I am brave enough to see
That Christ was not nailed up for me.

Yet when I'm old and flat in bed
Shall I be flesh enough to scorn
The prayers of friends, as those have done?
The candles haloing me dead?

WHEN I WAS A BIRD

When I was a bird, I was afraid
    Of the gods of the world.
When I was a bird, the sun drove me,
And the wind, to a cave of the dark and cold;
    And I
Was god of the cave.

My love was of worms; the stretch of the walls
    Was the stretch of my will.
My love was of worms, and of blind fish;
They were afraid; I was alone.
    And I
Was the will of their dark.

But the wind and the sun had fashioned my heart
    To be driven by gods.
The wind and the sunshine drew me again
To the world of gods and a memory of cold—
    When I
Was a bird, was a bird.

LEONARD NATHAN

Leonard E. Nathan writes that "I was born in 1924 in Los Angeles, California, served in the army in World War II, and got most of my education at the University of California at Berkeley where I now teach. My wife and I have three children. I have written verse from the time I was fifteen or so. These early efforts tended to the epic genre; my later work has been shorter and has appeared in a variety of magazines, among them: *Poetry, Accent, Kenyon Review, New Republic, Antioch Review, The Nation, The New Yorker, Western Review, Perspective,* and *The Quarterly Review.*

In 1958, the Talisman Press published a small volume of my verse, called *Western Reaches;* and in that same year I received the Phelan Award for narrative verse. In 1961, I received a Longview Foundation Award for some poems. My second volume of poems, *Glad And Sorry Seasons,* was published this spring by Random House. I am now working on two new books of verse, one for adults and one for children, although the chances are that they'll get mixed up before I'm through.

Like most poets, I write as I can, revise much, and hope that my ear has improved with age."

EPITHALAMION

No spilling armloads of roses or great-necked swans
Rode with the heart into this marriage day.
There was no subtle feeling for great lawns
Or dancing down a barbarous rose-spread way.

It was a simple time, the flesh obscured
Behind gray suits and modest women's fashion.
Thoughts of bedroom gracefully deferrred,
The house was proof from all unruly passion.

It is a quieter day; belief is a sad
Middle-class deference to a doubtful god.
Nothing about the affair was very bad
Or good, no one invited who was odd.

THE HIGHWAY

In that town, the Golden Highway
Ended at the just-now-built
El Royal Motel where I was lodged
For one night's luxurious loneness;
Early next morning, on the balcony
Overlooking a swimming pool glossed by wind,
I mused coldly on the green water
And the locked-up sleepers who later would warm it;
And when, in my used-up room, I repacked
And snapped shut the suitcase, the pool flashed
In my mind like a signal winking through sleep;
Through sleep also came the truckers grinding on
Toward their coffee stops, towering by
In their tall cabs, looking down, alone;
And alone I left, but—with the high vigilance
Of truckers—took from sleep its warmth;
From water, its green-wind dawn; from going,
A way to leave without goodby.

MAN AND WIFE

It's not admitted, but the thing they did
In spring's tall mustard, shadowed by the hill,
Was never equalled, though themselves they've said
The later mellow labor's better still.

I say it's never so and have the proof,
For they are now gentle, kind, and keep good rule
Within their house, who, when they had no roof,
Rose from the dawn like twins, divine and cruel.

SATISFACTION

When I crossed the river by bridge, I wrote down
In an empty matchbook: the river is nearly dry.

When I crossed the mountain range, I noted down
In a pocket-sized map: this grade has been made easy.

When I came to a desert gas station, I scribbled out
In a copy of *The Resurrection*: all comforts are here.

Beyond, a lizard outstared me in Arizona,
And the Navahos kept to their reservation.

But there must, oddly, be something left over beyond,
Though little enough; we've put that into the law.

Live and let live, my father used to shout
And, driving, loved to get lost — and, driving, failed.

STATE

My mind to me no kingdom is,
Good gradient from high to low,
Crowned order gently down to stone
From which God's saving waters flow;

Or even that democracy
Arranged by cool and shapely reason
Whose bust resembles Jefferson's
And whose revolts are in good season.

It is this rabble wandering wastes
Of foreign powers; its faithless head
Has neither talked to God nor heard
One good cause for having led.

APOLOGIA

Of you at our party, dear, of her, of those
Who circled toasts and danced a generous measure,
Then laughed to separate and laughed to close,
And had a time exchanging gentle pleasure,

Of all that company I wanted much
To praise, including me, the good we hide,
And, backing off, I gave up singling touch
To own them whole and from a dark aside.

But, friends, I found a thief on every hand
As though fond skin disguised a foreign make
Of beast whose pawing little strokes seemed planned
To find the combination and to take.

Dear one, somewhere between the lines above
I met myself returning pinched with love.

FATHER AND DAUGHTER

Little now, she's yours, and though she cries
At anger, her whole small heart consents to be
Your darling beyond her pleasure or her pain.
And it's so simple to be good and wise,
You can't see any end. But, though she's plain,
She'll pity you that loved too easily
What she, dressed like a woman for disguise,
Will carry, secret, through unfriendly rain
To him who waits upon her mystery.

TO ONE WHO LOST HER SON

Cannot be spoken words, cannot;
Not pictures, not the grave abstract;
Although these close with loss somewhat,
They cannot swallow fact.

Cannot be much, alone with this:
The missing full of love resigned,
The heart beat hollow, miles of grass,
The lumpish, lolling mind.

Cannot be others, though they pray
That yours can rest within their hurt.
Advice they cannot try you take . . .
They move; you are inert.

Can be this only: a rude grief.
Like mourning stone, reads at the brain
Intelligence it must believe,
Illiterate of pain.

AFTERMATH OF A LOSS

What won't be known must still be someway said,
Must find the words that suffer the event:
Face after face withdrawn, such old defection,
That darkness seems alive with what has fled.
One way to set it down is indirection;
Old Japanese, patient and reticent,
Drew it from the stag's autumnal cry,
The blank pillow, a creaking turn of leaf,
The way the wind utters the callous grass.
Of course, this is desperation with an eye
To ending dragon lengths of poison grief
Which move so slow, they may not ever pass.

CROP DUSTER

As obsolete as heroes, he takes flight
By straining wooden wings and toothpick struts;
Taut wire and box-like fuselage resist
All motion, though the rusty engine butts
Unclouded heaven, hammering at height
Until the whining propeller hurts to twist.
Now he banks lower on infected green
To harrow life that kills, though all life dies;
Then, staggering straight, he levels out to dust.
I see him now, his goggles like gross eyes
To take on earth the fix of his machine,
The life and death contraption of his trust.

IN THE PEACH ORCHARD: I

In the gray humidity of the winter orchard,
In the thin, lean-branched humidity
Of the fruitless orchard, to move is to be tense.
To be living under a dead light
And shade, a figure in shadow,
Is not movement but defining barely
In the twig-stopped wind, edging.

This is endurance.

Figure the muscled bud forcing
Outward redness within whiteness,
Until within the waste of white frost,
And the last flush of rain,
It issues, being tender,
All over the unleaved orchard, and all
That storm of blossom (let loose)
Breaks, outward over earth. To be now
Is to promise.

IN THE PEACH ORCHARD: II

In the green humidity of the unripe orchard,
In the unthinned, heavy-branched humidity
Of the green peaches, to move is to be green,
To be going under the green light
And shade, a figure of unreadiness,
Is not movement but conceiving slow
In the leaf-stopped wind, stifled.

This is promise.

Figure the stone peach forcing
Outward greenness through greenness,
Until from under the last layer of leaves,

And the last stretch of skin
It issues, being golden,
At the edge of the orchard and all
That green tempest (withheld)
Breaks, leaved and golden, downward: to move now
Is to fall.

AFTER THE FLOOD

Like ants twisting from a sudden mud
Slowly working back to solid land,
The people twist over the sinking flood,
And like the ants they barely understand.

The silt-sunk bed, the rain-burst chest of drawers,
The futile armchair, tilted and absurd,
Were never meant to suffer the outdoors,
So men move gravely, saying not a word.

The gull's flight through the swamped December sky
Became erratic in the thick of air
And someone should have heard that shocking cry
But human silence drowned it everywhere.

WINGS

The fragmentary birds confess
Within the branching heart of leaves
That every answered song retrieves
Absence between their singleness.

The rush of wings is deep to feel
When something stirs beyond mere sight
Uttering the much concealed in flight;
The unseen whole, Ezekiel's wheel.

FUNERAL FOR EMILY

The look on the face would never let me go
As if the withering distance came to be
All the nearness I could ever know
And that was just enough eternity
To make me crazy for my little time,
Me shout, me jump, me move, me anything
To show no kinship to this cold sublime
That peeped from under blossoms reeking spring.

A shape that has no breath,
Wax fruit in a basket
Smiles in the huge casket:
There's nothing quite like death.
A girl named Emily,
Dead these years and years,
Taught this trick to me;
She talks on, never tears,
Telling how far removed
Eternity has proved.
Her immortality
Is terrible to hear.

I dream myself so little, I don't care
For any thing I know will not survive,
And run into the darkness, meeting there
Dear Emily, who eats me up alive.

ORPHEUS AGAIN AND AGAIN

Like a compulsive, dreaming his fall once more,
He goes back down to make his song
And rescue from the dark
His imagined bride,
And fail
At the door
Because he'll long
To make certain that his work
Commands such power, or simple pride
Turns him to prove his talent's for the real.

And is almost; it's always at the mouth
Of bringing forth, but like his lyre,
Dies at the edge of stillness.
So Eurydice
Rests deep
In death;
No summoning power
Reaches beyond the mere fullness
Great song betrays; reality
Is one look more: Hades' undreamt sleep.

ANNUNCIATION

No fox *out there* has just that bark . . .
The midnight vineyard, gone to fog,
Is dumb again; hair on my neck
Lies slowly down. That was no dog
Or any beast who bore a name.

One summer noon I almost met
In the greenest midshade of the vines,
Where no one dreamed It might be yet,
The Marvel ripening at its ease;
The scent that Presence left behind
Was must—a foreign essence, true,
But not unfriendly to my kind.

I let it fade, but kept good faith
Until this night, estranged in foam,
Was summoned up to bark: *out there*
Is nothing, no-one, never home.

RETURN OF THE NATIVE

My people again moving in dark doorways:
Who can survive these greetings? Bent and handled
As candelabra in the bottom drawer,
Their features walk at you in the gross ruin
Of eachness. Hands extend, bare-branched from foreign
Smelling sleeves, from the black sleeves of the old country.

They motion from the knee-deep of thick speech
How they have heard your get-away into green
And bright distance, sudden in the sun to be
American and quick in smart abstraction
From their dense bent. They labor meanings
Of themselves, relating the imponderable
As a language of thick fingers and love, asking,
"You are the end to our old testament?"